LARRY LARSEN

BASS TACTICS

How You Can Catch More and Bigger Bass

by Larry Larsen

by Larsen's Outdoor Publishing

ISBN 0-936513-27-6

Library of Congress 92-74325

Published by:

LARSEN'S OUTDOOR PUBLISHING
2640 Elizabeth Place
Lakeland, FL 33813
(813) 644-3381

Illustrated by:
John Klein
Win Publishing
P.O. Box 206
Hudson, MI 49247

PRINTED IN THE UNITED STATES OF AMERICA

3 4 5 6 7 8 9 10

LIBRARY   ANNOTATION

Title: Larry Larsen On Bass Tactics	Sports & Recreation Fishing
Series: Larsen On Bass	799.1
Author: Larry Larsen	
Publisher: Larsen's Outdoor Publishing	LCCN: 92-74325
Copyright: 1993	ISBN: 0-936513-27-6

ADULT SMALL PRESS	
From a well-known outdoors journalist, "Larry Larsen On Bass Tactics" focuses on productive tactics that fool largemouth bass throughout the country. It offers numerous "how-to" tips and tricks that will help the reader catch more bass on his very next trip. Special features include hundreds of "bulleted" facts and illustrations that detail new and highly productive tactics.	Table of Contents Index B&W Illustrations Photographs ** Author Credentials ** He's America's most widely read bass fishing writer and author. More than 1,500 of Larsen's articles have appeared in magazines, including Outdoor Life, Sports Afield, and Field & Stream. Larsen has now authored 15 books on bass fishing and contributed chapters to another eight.
224 pages Paperbound	

Larry Larsen on Bass Tactics

Larry Larsen On Bass Tactics

CONTENTS & TROPHIES

(cont'd)

CONTENTS & TROPHIES (cont'd)

(cont'd)

CONTENTS & TROPHIES (cont'd)

SHORT STRIKES

Larry Larsen on Bass Tactics

ACKNOWLEDGEMENTS

I want to thank my friends in the fishing industry; the writers, editors, manufacturers, retailers, professional anglers and guides and most of all, the individuals that have helped me become a better fisherman, writer and book author. On-the-water experiences with many people over the past 30 years have helped hone my angling skill, and communication via mail, fax, computer modem, phone, audio and video tape have contributed to my development and presentation of copy within these pages.

Thanks to John Klein of Hudson, MI, whose illustrations contributed greatly to the unique design of "Larry Larsen On Bass Tactics". The line drawings allow easy understanding of the tactics and concepts presented within the copy. I appreciate the valuable contribution of my wife, Lilliam, and our assistant Jennifer Forsthoefel. Their editing and production assistance is much appreciated.

I also want to thank the serious bass fishermen of the world - those who yearn for more information resulting in more strikes on the water. I have met many knowledgeable and eager consumers of book information at my seminars and promotions and appreciate their kind words of encouragement to keep writing books on bass!

Larry Larsen on Bass Tactics

PREFACE

"Larry Larsen On Bass Tactics" focuses on productive tactics that fool largemouth bass throughout the country. The book, dedicated to serious bass anglers, is drenched with "how-to" tips and tricks. Those readers who are interested in learning about the sport will catch more bass on their very next trip.

- Literally, hundreds of "bulleted" facts will benefit the anglers, regardless of their skill level. This is the most detailed approach to presenting bass tactics ever offered.

- More than 70 line drawings and photos carefully illustrate and detail new and highly productive tactics. The drawings allow easy understanding of the tactics and concepts presented.

This book, "Larry Larsen On Bass Tactics," will be a valuable reference source with carefully detailed steps and illustrations for the tactics presented. The tips within each chapter will make a better fisherman of all.

- The proven techniques discussed by Larry are applicable to all bass waters around the country.

- The reader will find numerous interesting concepts and ideas within the pages of this book to try the next time he is on the water.

As catching several fish on each trip grows tougher and tougher, the reader will find knowledge and encouragement in this book to make that next venture to the lake or stream more successful. The steps to go back out on the water "armed" with the latest information are carefully delineated.

For anglers who want to learn to be better bass fishermen and to enjoy their fishing more, "Larry Larsen On Bass Tactics" casts directly in their direction. Those that study this guide to expand their knowledge will be setting the hook much more often this year!

CHAPTER 1

INTRODUCTION - THE ULTIMATE "HOW-TO"
What's in store for those who study

This book is not about colorful experiences that paint moods as starting points for your daydreaming. "Larry Larsen On Bass Tactics" is a "how-to" book, pure and simple. Sure there are anecdotes sprinkled throughout, but they are used to carefully illustrate a point. You will learn from each experience presented, because it is there to either prove or clarify tactical statements and decisions.

You'll find numerous explicit discussions and bulleted highlights of Larry's reasoning for the tactics presented. On each page of this book, you'll either learn something new or have your existing knowledge strongly reinforced, so much that it will be motivational in helping you catch more bass.

The detailed explanations in the text are only part of the information developed to help you catch bigger bass and in greater numbers. The superb illustrations are all highlights of additional information about each topic. Each requires a minimum of study effort, and the results will be proven on your next trip to the lake.

"Larry Larsen On Bass Tactics" has been written as an informational guide for outlining specific tactics to catching more and bigger bass.

What You'll Find In This Book

There are 29 additional chapters in "Larry Larsen On Bass Tactics" that are dedicated to serious bass anglers - those who are truly interested in learning about the sport. You'll find the information of use on your very next trip to the lake.

In Chapters 2, 3, and 4, you'll learn how to catch more bass from aquatic vegetation. The coverage varies from selecting the most promising plant community, to specialized tactics for a variety of floating, emergent and submergent vegetation. Tricks and techniques for specific circumstances in "weed holes" are detailed.

You'll learn how to develop a systematic approach to fishing any type of vegetation. Duck weed, hyacinth and other thickets pose problems that you'll be able to solve most every time out. Clues on bird traffic will reveal how they relate to bass locations. Fishing concentrations in the towering plants, boat positioning, drawing strikes, fishing mats and selecting the right lures are discussed. The essentials for providing proper lure action and control in the densest vegetation are presented.

When you finish Chapters 5, 6, and 7, you'll know the most effective methods for locating and catching bass in deep waters during the cooler months and in clear waters throughout the year. You'll learn how to fish heated waters, how fronts affect such waters, and how fronts affect the fishing in them. Overlooked yet deadly lures are revealed, along with the specialized tactics and ideal locations to employ them. You'll learn how the most productive tactics vary from normally-clear waters to those that are clear only occasionally (seasonally). Detailed also are the baits and basics of clear water bass fishing.

In Chapters 8 through 11, you'll discover new and highly productive tactics for fishing small waters. You'll learn the best ways to locate bass in the tiny ponds and creeks, and you'll find out how to finesse bass from such environments. The right craft, boat positioning and approach and other keys to catching bass in tight places and mini-habitats are discussed. You'll learn where to look for prime ultra-light spots, and what is most effective. Urban bass opportunities are detailed, from gaining access, approaching the right structure and rigging for development waters.

Chapters 12 through 15 tell you what you need to know about fishing in the wind and trolling for bigger fish. You'll learn tactical details on boat positioning, trolling motor operation, anchor use and dragging, keeping a lure in the strike zone, lure selection and presentation in strong windy conditions. Trolling through highly-vegetated bodies of water is often avoided, but you'll learn some secrets to maneuvering and repositioning over bass. Speed variations and repeatability, equipment, buoy marking, and sizing the bait and line are all discussed in detail.

In Chapters 16 through 19, you'll learn the most productive ploys for catching bass when wade fishing or float fishing. The best areas to employ these tactics are delineated. You'll learn how to

Larry Larsen on Bass Tactics

analyze the water, "launch" selection, approach a wadeable area, and select the right lures. A detailed treatment of map consultation is offered, as is a review on how to select belly boats. Tactics to most effectively work an area from a tube or wade position are presented. What to do and not to do when getting wet for bass are pointed out. Creature and weather considerations, plus safety points are detailed.

    Chapters 20 to 23 tell you tactics that the author employs on his two favorite types of bass-laden areas: docks and runoffs. You'll learn how to fish waterfalls, spillways, dams, runoffs and other discharges to catch large numbers of fish. The most effective lure presentations and techniques, unique and secret strategies and current fishing tips are detailed. You'll know the key bass concentrating factors in runoffs and below man-made structures. Find out the "sweeteners" to look for around docks and boat houses, and you'll catch more fish focusing on those particular habitats.

    Chapters 24 through 30 provide detailed tactics for solving some "minor problems" such as adverse weather, inactive bass, crowded waters, darkness and fluctuating water chemistry and temperatures. You'll learn the best "frontal" response for lock-jaw bass and how to catch suspended and pre-spawn bass.

The various types of tree "relief" and how to catch fish from them is discussed. How fishing pressure affects bass and how you can adjust to catch them is explained. You'll find out how to select the best lakes for moonless angling and how to fish them productively. Six vegetation-specific methods for night fishing are detailed. Finally, you'll learn how water temperature wisdom can be applied year around.

Once you finish studying the figures and text in "Larry Larsen on Bass Tactics", you can further enhance your knowledge and information library by obtaining the 9-volume BASS SERIES LIBRARY. The valuable library is available at many sporting goods, fishing tackle shops and book stores. You can also order an autographed set directly from the publisher (information is in the Resource Directory at the back of this book).

Don't let people tell you that catching big fish and catching a lot of them is luck. KNOWLEDGE AND ITS WISE USE IS THE KEY TO CATCHING BIGGER AND MORE BASS - Larry Larsen

Larry Larsen on Bass Tactics

CHAPTER 2
FLOATING PLANT STRATEGIES
How to attract more bass from under surface canopies

The birds were there, some feeding on small bugs and worms and others picking out grass shrimp and minnows. Our bobbers sat at the edge of the thick, floating hyacinth canopy on which herons, egrets and other water birds walked.

I had anchored at the shallow creek bend after noticing the bird life moving over the aquatic jungle. Food was undoubtedly being jarred from those plants, and while the feathered flock explored the tops of the hyacinth clog, small panfish and minnows were attracted to the root base. I was sure of that.

As I soon found out, my hunch about largemouth also being present proved true. My eight-inch shiner frantically tried to "climb out" onto the floating mat as an eight-pounder boiled the surface behind it. The bass' second attempt was successful, and I watched the cork disappear under the surface.

I engaged the reel and set the hook in time to stop the fish from burying itself 30 feet back under the cover. Soon the bass was worked free of the hanging plant obstructions and was landed. That fish and three more of lesser weight were caught and subsequently released back into the canopy.

Certain floating plants, like hyacinths, water lettuce, pennywort, and duckweed, make great surface canopies and provide tremendous bass habitat.

Develop A Systematic Approach

Regardless of the floating vegetation type, waters under such canopies are, indeed, the home of many largemouth. If the right

Floating Plant Strategies   17

habitat and water characteristics exist, most of the bass population may be there. Developing a systematic approach to consistently locate largemouth is the key to catching bass in such places.

Certain techniques produce in some aquatic plants, while completely different tactics may be optimal for others. Floating plants demand specific tactics.

Surprisingly, even large bass can be easily worked out from under most floating vegetation. Hyacinths, lettuce, duckweed, smartweed and the smaller-leafed pennywort don't pose too many problems to anglers. Why? The favorite bass holding structures are, after all, on or near the surface. Will they remain a favorite? Look at this:

- Floating plants send off shoots from a main root system, and when separated, will form a second root system and a second plant. They propagate quickly.

- The floating qualities of such plants enable them to spread by wind and currents, where they can quickly cover excellent shallow bass-holding structure.

- Crayfish, bugs, grass shrimp, insects and other forage are abundant in and below the dense floating mats. Bass and other game fish often feed under the shaded canopy.

A predominant wind on some lakes will result in a "floating skin" that is fairly tough to penetrate with a lure. The canopy actually secures the watery environment. The largemouth can freely roam beneath the cover and seek out forage, seemingly without apprehension.

Don't Overlook Duckweed Canopies

Every cast gets fouled in the tiny floating cover called duckweed. Even when a big bass explodes through it with his mouth wrapped around a plug, the aquatic plant is right in the middle of the action. Never mind though; largemouth don't seem to be overly concerned about it.

The constant plant "pest" that adorns each lure or bait reeled to the boat is one-eighth inch in diameter, sitting on the water's surface and drifting with the wind. The microscopic, hair-like root structure on the wet side of each plant is not long enough to intertwine, so duckweed must be considered as thousands of independently floating plants.

Wind can concentrate floating plants into coves or lake arms, and pegged worms flipped to dense floating cover can be very productive. The author believes in getting up close and personal with weed-bound bass.

Several factors enter into establishing a successful pattern with the "green blanket"-loving largemouth. Check out the following:

- Weather - Full sun means the bass may be concentrated beneath the canopy.

- Lake-bottom characteristics - Cover in the form of submerged trees and vegetation stalks means bass may be concentrated.

- Forage availability - The type of predominant forage affects the appropriate tackle selection and the most productive presentations. Match the size of the forage and the action.

Duckweed exists on numerous waters around the country. While it may not be commonly found in some parts, it is a fantastic find for those able to unlock its treasures.

How To Solve Hyacinth Problems

It doesn't take long for hyacinths to spread by propagation. For example, a single water hyacinth plant is capable of producing 50,000 new plants each year. The floaters, found throughout shallow waters in the southern half of the U.S., attract aquatic activity, which is a good sign. The best combination of aquatic life, according to many guides, is turtles, frogs, alligators and hyacinths. Turtle activity is important because they feed after a forage spree by the bass.

Crankbaits that resemble crayfish, a favorite forage of bass, are a good choice around hyacinths. The plants are loaded with grass shrimp and small crayfish. Here's how to fish the lures:

- Cast behind a hyacinth jam and bring the lure out underneath a corner. Bass will often stop it just as it leaves the shade. The wind or current will help make the right cast and control the retrieve.

- Points that are formed by the plant, as well as cuts through them, can be productive. Some anglers take their paddles and "notch" the weeds. After making a series of pockets in the cover, they back off and either cast lures or allow tail-hooked shiners to swim into the notches.

- Cast the lure so that you can work it under the canopy as far as possible. Casts to a floating weed line may result in a few bass, but the large concentrations are well back under the stuff.

Anglers often are lazy and won't try to figure out the best way to reach the fish under those circumstances. That's why there are so many largemouth in such places.

Fishing the weed hole thickets can be tough, extremely tough. Some waters are weedy, but they're also bassy. Usually, the bass can be caught, regardless of how much vegetation exists.

- Throwing a large topwater plug over floating aquatic weeds to work open water behind them is one effective ploy. The surface bait is often best for such habitat because it allows the angler to present it precisely and slowly to the onlookers under or in the perimeter vegetation.

The weed hole wasn't large, spanning only 20 feet or so, but it was promising. Floating vegetation cornered by dead tree tops projecting above the water level rimmed one side of the small

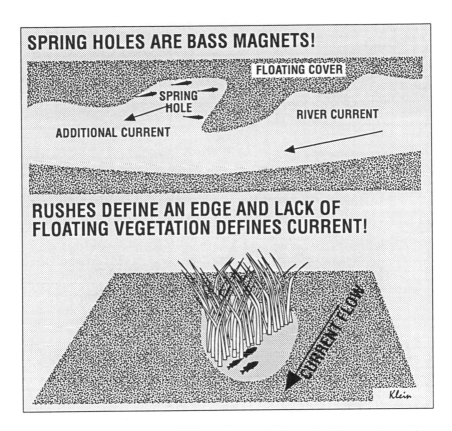

SPRING HOLES ARE BASS MAGNETS!

FLOATING COVER

SPRING HOLE

RIVER CURRENT

ADDITIONAL CURRENT

RUSHES DEFINE AN EDGE AND LACK OF FLOATING VEGETATION DEFINES CURRENT!

CURRENT FLOW

Klein

target. It was at least 15 feet deep, with probably an irregular bottom. I had encountered what I felt was great bass territory.

My cast over 20 feet of vegetation landed strategically at the edge of the hyacinths on the far side of the open water. I began to gently twitch the big topwater plug toward the weeds on the nearside of the hole. I figured that my probe would draw interest from a bass cruising the shadowy skirts of the open water. My thoughts hadn't yet turned to how I might get a hooked fish out of there.

The Zara Spook was nearing the edge of the hole when it disappeared in a huge boil. Hyacinths at the edge of the open water seemed to blow up, as I put all the power that I dared into the seven-foot heavy action rod. The bass was apparently too big to haul out over the vegetation back to the boat. I had to go after her.

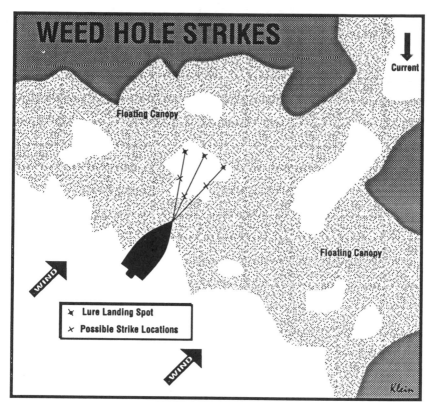

Holes in floating vegetation provide small open water targets. Casts over vegetation to the potholes should land strategically at the rim of the plants on the far side of the open water. The slow moving bait should be retrieved near the edge of the weeds along either side of the hole. That will often draw interest from bass cruising the shadowy skirts of the open water. Strikes will probably occur at the nearside edge of the pothole.

There's Only One Way To Get To The Fish

I flipped the trolling motor switch to 24 volts and smashed the button while struggling with the baitcasting outfit. The fish resisted the extra pressure for awhile and then tried to make like a bird. It shot through the surface mat and fell back into the vegetation. That made the entanglement even worse.

REVEALING BIRD TRAFFIC

Birds are a key to finding some of the better weed hole thickets where large bass lurk. A productive angler will be aware of bird traffic. If there are birds feeding and walking around on the aquatic jungle, then there must also be small bugs, worms, etc. in those plants. Usually, the older mat of plants will offer more food.

Insect-hunting birds may tip you off to both the bait fish and the bass. Egrets and herons working a shallow flat near a plant jungle usually means minnows are present also between and beneath the plants, where the larger fish can get at them. Coots and ibis are frequent feeders on eel grass and other vegetation, and they are birds to watch, although almost any kind of activity around the plants is a good sign.

Another reason to fish such areas is that lunkers eager for a feathered meal may be present. Bass will definitely attack small birds when possible, and I've seen some swirls and splashes beneath birds tip-toeing along over the water plants. Usually, the bass will miss their targets, but if you're quick, you can get a cast in close to the action and maybe score on the predator.

The electric on the bow of my boat was slowly "eating" its way through the weed canopy fortress between me and the six-pound largemouth. As I neared the area, I stopped the electric motor and kneeled to hand-pick the clumps of hyacinths encompassing my fish. Grabbing the floating vegetation and its water-soaked root structure, I eagerly threw aside those plants that were not a part of the fish entanglement. I finally found the fish.

The fish was my third from the weed thickets that morning. This one, the biggest, also was the most difficult to get at. My boat ended up with four or five wet plants tossed into the interior and its bow pointed into the hole. The easiest way to get it back out was to start the outboard engine, turn around by jockeying it in the weed hole, and motoring out through the semblance of a path partially cleared by the electric motor.

You'll catch a lot of giant largemouth from such spots. For further information on specialized trophy bass techniques, you may want to check out "Trophy Bass" which is book 7 in the Bass Series Library.

Wind-Blown Weed Holes

Floating plants often spread until they are trapped or contained, but fortunately, the bass productivity of the water increases until the vegetation coverage exceeds 30 percent of the acreage, according to some fishery reports. Floating plants can be all-encompassing, but sometimes, productive open surface water can be found. Here are a couple of great spots to check:

- One place is often around limited flow creeks just off a main body of water. The current will keep the hole open and allow the angler an opportunity to cast such places.

- The best areas to begin a search on most lakes with floating cover are usually the deeper waters where vegetation exists. If there is a predominant wind in the area, then start your search on the windward shoreline.

A wind can pile plenty of the floating plants into coves or lake arms and, thanks to the containment aspects of other emergent cover, pockets of open water may exist. Check out these types of waters first, and you'll usually stay with them the rest of the day.

CHAPTER 3

TRICKS FOR TOWERING GUARDIANS

How to fish the toughest masses of emergent vegetation

Tall emergent vegetation, such as bulrushes, cattails and reeds, offers bass heavy cover in which to bury themselves. The dense stands of aquatic weeds that often grow to eight feet above the surface are the home of many concentrations of largemouth.

While there are several productive methods for fishing emergent vegetation, one of the best is by flippin' or swinging a weedless lure into an opening in the stands. Many anglers back off from these stands, fearing constant hangups, but the "flippers" move their boats in tight to the cover and, while standing, wave their long, seven-foot rods in an effort to dunk their bait into a bass hideout. With practice, they learn to flip the lure in all potential pockets with few snags.

A weedless jig or Texas-rigged worm is employed in the technique, which consists of vertically jigging the lure up and down eight to 10 times in each hole in the stand.

- Begin the "yo-yo" type cast by raising the rod tip, keeping the bait just off the water's surface, while simultaneously stripping off more line with the left hand. With an underhand swing, arch the lure in a pendulum motion toward the target. The left hand should slow the lure's descent and allow it to drop noiselessly behind the rushes.

- The amount of line out at the end of the drop is usually less than 12 feet. When flippin' in heavy cover, try to let the lure hit the bottom directly in the middle of the weed hole. Once the lure has softly plummeted to the bottom in heavy vegetation, lift up on the rod lightly to determine if a bass might be in possession of the bait prior to jigging it up and down.

- For a shot at the largest bass, let the bait sit still for 10 seconds before checking it. Lift it up slowly, and then, let it fall back to the bottom again. Let the bait sit once again for several seconds. You might have to do that three or four times to entice a trophy bass.

When the bass are concentrated in shallow water under thickly matted reeds, it is possible to catch three or four largemouth from a single hole. There are a couple of very important tricks to maximize the catch when using the flippin' worm rig:

1. In such dense cover, the slip sinker cannot be left to free-slide. It must be pegged by inserting a round toothpick into the sinker and breaking off the tip to wedge the line and weld the worm and weight together.

2. The worm should be oiled heavily with a fish attractor solution to facilitate sliding it in and out of the weed stands.

How To Catch More Than Your Share

Some emergent plants, like spatterdock and fragrant water lilies, can grow into masses of vegetation so thick that only a few small pockets exist. This is where a conventional cast and retrieve may be more appropriate. The light below is subdued, but a lure's movement above does not go unnoticed. If the bait is kept moving across the weeds, it will attract attention.

Lily pad or bonnet beds often have pockets or holes to fish. The best approach to use there is to toss an extremely weedless bait that can be fished slowly. Fat plastic baits, plastic spoons, snake imitations and other rubber lures may be most suitable. They will draw some exciting strikes from the thickets and yet work free of most pad entanglements.

To effectively catch more than your share while casting offerings, position the boat close to the shallow weed mass that you intend to fish. Your overhand, sidearm or underhand cast should still be fairly short, so that you can maintain a good degree of accuracy and proper control of the lure as it is being retrieved. Two factors are in play here:

1. Dense cover allows you to move in tighter on the quarry.

2. The odds of landing the bass improve as the line length decreases.

Boat Position Is Vital To Success

The boater can generally move his craft into and over such vegetated areas without disturbing the entire area. Often, though, a small canoe or john boat may be less noticeable to the inhabitants. Minimize the use of the electric motor while within the

Larry Larsen on Bass Tactics

SHADOWS ON THE WEEDS
Moving shadows scare bass

Shadows moving ahead of flippers

Klein

weedbed; the prop will hit plant stalks, causing vibration waves to spread until dampened by the surrounding weeds.

How To Attract The Strike In Pad Beds

The weed pockets are where the majority of strikes will occur. The steps to generating a strike are easy.

- Cast a weedless lure beyond the target opening to avoid spooking any nearby inhabitant.

- Inch the lure to the edge of the pocket and let it free fall to the bottom. Most strikes will occur on the fall.

- Watch the lure as it crawls along on top of the mass and the line when the bait falls.

As I've said, weedless jig and eels are sometimes effective in this shallow habitat, and of course, the weedless spoon has a well-deserved reputation for attracting weed-bound largemouth. Don't

Shallow water vegetation is the home of most bass in a body of water containing such. Forage opportunities are abundant and largemouth grow fat around the "food shelf". Rigid emergent vegetation can hide a tremendous bass fishery within.

worry about getting hung up, worry about hanging onto the rod when the bait drops into a pocket.

What Should You Look For In A Mass Of Vegetation?

Heavy cover often replaces depth in the requirements of bass. Tall, shoreline weed beds provide bass with security of sorts and plenty of forage. To the bass, it is an enticing, food-intensive environment that provides shallow ambush cover.

- Areas where the weeds are different in some way are particularly active bass haunts. An expanse of maidencane with an isolated patch or two of pickerel weed is an example. The bass would most probably concentrate in the dense pickerel patch.

- The successful caster will check out points, boat lanes and clearing in and around shallow weed masses.

How To Draw Strikes In Grasses

Dense patches of peppergrass, Johnson grass or other "soft" emergent vegetation with assorted potholes are superb habitat for lunker largemouth. Most grasses lean with the wind or waves.

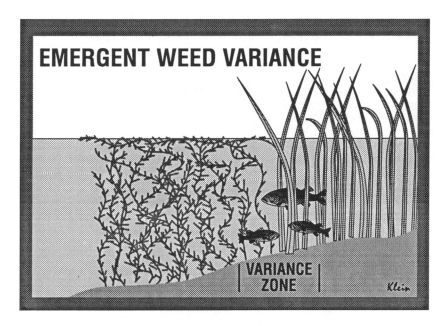

EMERGENT WEED VARIANCE

VARIANCE ZONE

A weed variance, the zone where vegetation type changes from one to another, is a prime spot for bass. Check out any variance.

Their sparse growth is interspersed with areas of open water. Bass work through the vegetation and also tend to hang out around the edges of such cover.

Surface spinnerbaits, noisy spoons and buzz-type lures create the disturbance necessary to attract largemouth from their lair within the grass.

CAST-AND-RETRIEVE - Casts with the weedless fare can be made to almost any spot, but the retrieve should bring the bait back over the open water pockets in the grass. Fish the lures slowly and near or on the surface for maximum action.

STRIKES - Strikes will normally occur near the open water areas, but beware of the actively feeding bass in the denser grass. If they have a chance at the lure and are quick enough, you may have a battle on your hands.

THE FIGHT - Keeping the bass head up with the aid of a stout rod's leverage is often vital to landing the fish.

Not All Towering Plants Provide The Same Habitat

Rigid emergent vegetation can hide a tremendous bass fishery within, but not all plants are alike in terms of habitat. Cattails have leaves that branch off as they rise from the water's surface and grow in relatively shallow water. They also grow in extremely dense masses with each stalk an inch or so from its neighbor, and seldom have pockets within.

Bulrushes, on the other hand, often have small areas of open water between its clumps. The 'buggy whips' are also easier to fish because they are stiff and straight, and bass prefer the additional protection from such "high-rise" reeds.

As earlier presented in my book, "Shallow Water Bass" (book 5 in the BASS SERIES LIBRARY), emergent vegetation in the most fertile soil will grow to be the tallest and most productive. Chapter 8 entitled "Larsen's Flora Factor" reveals a 10-step analysis for determining the best community of vegetation to fish. Reading it will provide you with the best available information on the subject.

Larry Larsen on Bass Tactics

CHAPTER 4

BREAKING INTO HYDRILLA HIDEOUTS
How to Fish Submergent Plant Life That You Can't See

In today's world, you had better be able to employ the right methods to effectively fish submergent vegetation habitats, such as hydrilla, pepper grass, eel grass, elodea and coontail moss. To be highly productive each time out and have a trophy bass or two as your goal is not out of reason.

Some anglers struggle against overly abundant submerged vegetation in search of their quarry. Others utilize the knowledge of how bass interact with vegetation to catch more and larger bass. Equipment and methods to catch these bass under normal conditions can be unique.

Characteristics of lakes with submergent vegetation may vary. Some have relatively clear water while others sport darker, nutrient-intensive waters. Hydrilla may be the most common, as it's abundant in many waters throughout the country. In other waters, the predominant vegetation may be pepper grass, coontail or elodea, or a combination.

A drought in areas with highly-vegetated waters can take a toll on the influx of water and reduce the lake's clear, open areas. That usually plays havoc on access, but not on the fishing in the submergent plant communities.

Why are bass in the weedy thickets?

- They offer shelter for fish food organisms, shade, better pH levels and more moderate water temperatures. The sediment from submergent plants can pile up on the lake's bottom if the plants get

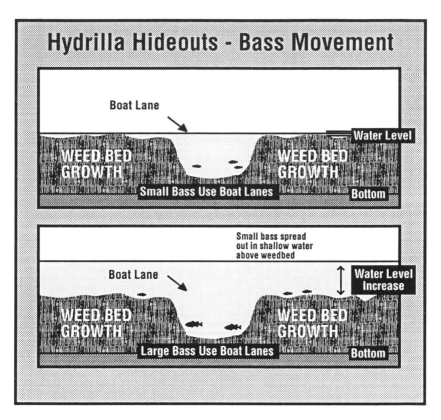

Hydrilla Hideouts - Bass Movement

Boat Lane

Water Level

WEED BED GROWTH

WEED BED GROWTH

Small Bass Use Boat Lanes

Bottom

Small bass spread out in shallow water above weedbed

Boat Lane

Water Level Increase

WEED BED GROWTH

WEED BED GROWTH

Large Bass Use Boat Lanes

Bottom

too populous and die off. The bottom sediment, though, warms up the water in the winter, while shade from the plant communities cools the water in the summer.

Check Out The Hydrilla Mats

Hydrilla, which often grows to the water's surface and then mats up, has spread throughout the states. But it provides fish with extraordinary cover. Hydrilla helps define existing structures in some cases. For example, a hydrilla weedline may establish the presence of a drop in depth due to a creek bed or river channel.

Thousands of acres of 'shag carpet' exist in lakes scattered around the United States. Hydrilla, a rooted plant, can survive in almost any weather and spread by fragmentation. Wind, waves and boaters cut and separate the soft upper shoots of this competitive plant, which re-establishes itself firmly. Small fragments on a boat trailer can be transplanted from one lake to another, and from state to state.

Dense patches of submergent vegetation often contain numerous potholes which offer superb habitat for largemouth. Bass that inhabit submergent vegetation tend to hang out in the holes or around the edges of such cover.

Although several lakes and coves of large reservoirs may be choked with mats of hydrilla, fishing usually improves. What was once a good bass lake is often transformed by hydrilla to a great lake, often increasing the fish population.

Use The Right Lure Action To Draw Attention

To attract the bass from the deep moss bed requires lures that can disturb the surface in a "natural" manner. Little movement is required to create a disturbance and produce some audible noise, because bass concealed in the shade of the submerged weed bed will carefully observe what is going on above them.

Breaking Into Hydrilla Hideouts

In the spring and fall months, surface baits are an excellent choice for a couple of reasons:

- Since the action and control of most surface lures is through the rod tip, a taut line and careful attention to the action are desirable for fishing heavy weed cover.

- Surface-worked lures on hydrilla-infested waters are what brings bass to the top, making it easier for the angler to keep the largemouth out of entanglements below. That is the key to landing them in this cover.

As the summer progresses, bass move back into the submerged moss. In the long, hot days, submergent aquatic plants often grow to the surface and then mat up. Catching bass from submerged plants then requires special methods. To be an effective producer in this cover, the weedless lure must ride the surface easily.

- Single-shaft spinners and spoons are very effective in heavy hydrilla cover. A single hook and the ability to ride the surface and bounce over small obstructions is the key to productivity. The lure design dictates its action, but the retrieve should begin just before the lure hits the water. Bass may follow it for several feet in the hydrilla-covered waters before pouncing on it.

- Buzzbaits with a blade design that easily pops it to the surface, allows the successful fisherman to retrieve it on top at a very slow pace. It can be used around dense moss and should be fished with the rod tip held high. Begin reeling just before the lure hits the water so that it is always on the surface.

Control Of The Lure Is The Key To Hook-Ups

In heavy vegetation bass will seldom have time to carefully examine the lure and will strike instinctively. Lunker bass are particularly hard to land from an aquatic jungle, but having a lure that will work well to provoke the strike is a major consideration. Once that is accomplished, you can work on getting her out of the entanglements.

Sinking lures or fast-moving baits used in such places would not be as easy to control. Surface baits also draw wakes that can give away the presence of an interested bass. Their methodical "call" seems to be highly effective in these particular areas.

Some Clear Water Approaches That Fool Bass

Angler success in clear, weed-bound waters can often depend on lure presentation distance. Soft-landing lures, thin-web lines, and long casts put fish in the boat on such waters.

CRANKBAITS IN HYDRILLA

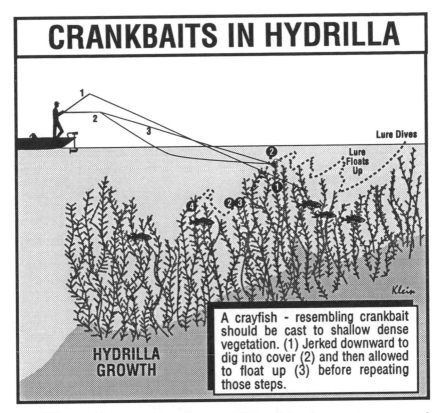

Lure Dives

Lure Floats Up

HYDRILLA GROWTH

A crayfish - resembling crankbait should be cast to shallow dense vegetation. (1) Jerked downward to dig into cover (2) and then allowed to float up (3) before repeating those steps.

The number one aquatic weed "pest" in clear waters around the country is probably hydrilla. It, like other submergent vegetation, grows better in certain soils and at certain depths. It will opt for clear, high-nutrient waters and shallow, soft bottoms. The topography of a lake is such that its composition varies and accordingly, so does the growth of the plant mass. Numerous pockets exist in the submergent vegetation, and all harbor bass.

Fishing the clear water of hydrilla holes can present some challenges and interesting solutions.

- Most highly-vegetated waters have soft lake bottoms, so you can't wade-fish them; you may disappear if you do. For that very reason, it may also be difficult to use a heavy bullet weight on a Texas-rigged worm.

- One of my favorite methods to take bass from the pockets of open water on a hydrilla-bound lake is the belly-hooked worm rig. You can use an extra long, medium action rod, 14-pound test monofilament and a weightless six-inch, high-flotation worm. The plastic wiggler is belly hooked, leaving the hook point exposed.

With the relatively limber rod, you can cast the funny-looking worm rig long distances to areas of extremely clear water among the submergent vegetation. Bass that would spook at the sound of heavier lures landing, heavier line or shorter casts, are yours for the taking. Several 10-pound-plus bass have fallen for this tactic.

Don't Overlook The Crankbait In And Around The Masses

In immense vegetation, it can be difficult to effectively fish lures other than topwater plugs or weightless worms. Crankbaits can be particularly troublesome under these conditions, but they can be effective.

- One way to attack the problem is by using deep-diving crankbaits and retrieving them over hydrilla-covered bottoms in a jigging fashion. Pull until the plug hits the weeds, drop the rod tip to allow the bait to float up off the grass, reel in the slack and then repeat the process.

- Strikes will normally occur as the crankbait pauses and begins its free ascent.

It takes great feel to successfully fish a crankbait this way, since you have to detect the difference between hydrilla growth and a largemouth sucking in the lure. That can be difficult as the lure floats free of a potential weed hangup.

BATTLING THE FISH AND ENVIRONMENT

Abundant emergent vegetation can make a shallow lake much more productive. Likewise, it can generate a much better fishery in a small pond. Waters with profuse aquatic plant life rising skyward are difficult to fish, but they often have lunkers that rule their territory. If you get one on, the brute may take advantage of his familiarity with the habitat to get off.

If the water is off-color or stained, it's possible to use fairly heavy tackle around thick cover, particularly if a wall mount is your only quarry. Graphite rods, like the Berkley Series One, and stout casting reels spooled with 20-pound test monofilament line are ideal to battle with trophy bass in such an environment.

With the base and root system of many aquatic weeds providing easy entanglements, a large bass shouldn't be given its head. I prefer to pull the fish away from heavy cover and fight it on my terms. Be prepared to do battle in and around weed hole thickets, and you'll have a lunker story to tell.

CHAPTER 5

THE DEEP - COLD FRONT ESCAPES

Cold weather may affect anglers, but not bass in the depths

Big bass living in deep water are "pattern" fish during times of cold water temperatures. Generally, what one does, all will do. So, smart anglers will concentrate on finding a school of largemouth.

Cold fronts affect shallow and deep water fish differently when cover exists in the littoral (shallow feeding) zone. High pressure and resulting clear skies may shut off the deep water fish. Bass concentrations will move away from structure then to suspend over even deeper water, and they can be difficult to locate.

Shallow water fish, on the other hand, are more likely to be individual fish and an approaching front will move them to the heaviest cover. Flippin' is a technique that can be effective then, but I still prefer to go after the larger groups in the deep. Deep water bass are normally larger and less affected by the front.

Two forms of safety exist for big bass: 1. Dense cover, and 2. Deep water.

Given a choice, winter bass prefer the second. Deep water is more stable environmentally, and the fish can frequent sharp ledges and creek channels in frigid times. Bass can move quickly when a norther' hits and secure themselves in deeper depths.

Why You Should Fish Deep Water

Finding bass in the depths can be a gold mine! Cold weather bass hold tighter to the bottom and to themselves, when concentrated. They are not as active in shallow water, so it is very important to search deep haunts. I have often caught bass in 30 to

45 feet of water during the winter months, and probably half of those fish exceeded four pounds.

There are a few considerations for catching such fish:

- Catching bass positioned on the deep points and humps in the dead of winter requires lures that run deep or easily fall to the bottom.

- Since bass are often inactive in cold water, you need to have a sensitive touch to detect the transmittal of an oft times very light strike.

- You must realize that cold weather does affect the water temperature and bass movements, even in the depths. A change of a few degrees can result in an entirely different catch. On southern lakes, for example, water temperatures may vary by five to eight degrees from one area of the lake to another.

Know How Temperature Variations Affect The Bass

Thermal variations are most easily noticed near the shores of larger lakes, but even small power plant lakes may have a severe temperature fluctuation from cove to cove. On Fayette County Lake in Texas, as an example, I found a range of surface water temperature from 54 degrees to 68 degrees (near the hot water outlet canal) one January day.

Another of my favorite power generating lakes, Calaveras near San Antonio, Texas, has two main arms where temperature may vary by some 10 to 12 degrees in mid-winter. Cold weather there usually pushes the schools of shad and other forage down, and the bass follow. Like many heated reservoirs, Calaveras' creek channels run to depths of 60 feet. This deep water is warmed by the power plant discharge, while the shallows are susceptible to cold fronts which push water temperatures down.

Power plant lakes in Texas and elsewhere throughout the country are, of course, affected by a warm-water discharge from the electric generating plant. Water entering power plants is usually heated to a temperature several degrees above that of the lake. This affects nearby coves and the circulating channel that is created between the discharge and the intake canals.

Where You Should Look On The Nearest Heated Water

Many bass haunts in heated deep waters are most productive once the sun has warmed the surface above them. Wind and rays

Larry Larsen on Bass Tactics

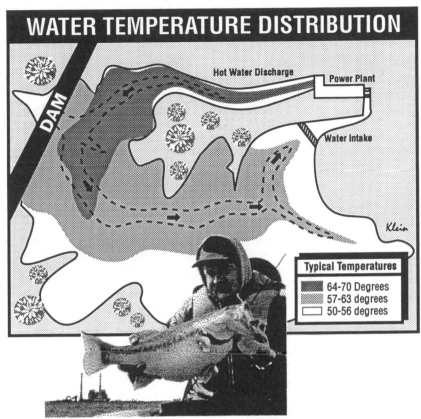

WATER TEMPERATURE DISTRIBUTION

Hot Water Discharge

Power Plant

DAM

Water Intake

Klein

Typical Temperatures

64-70 Degrees
57-63 degrees
50-56 degrees

Temperatures may vary from area to area by five to eight degrees in a non-heated lake and by 10 to 15 degrees in one affected by power plant discharges. Bass will seek out the warmest depths.

from the sun can have a significant effect on all waters, though, regardless of the presence of a heat source. Here's a few suggestions:

- Bass will often lie on rip rap near a dam around circulating canal jetties or on deep brush piles.

- A sun-drenched area protected from the wind may yield a markedly different catch than a deeper cove on the other end of the lake pounded by the wind.

Heated waters dispersed by strong southerly winds result in a more homogeneous lake. The water will warm gradually in the early spring, a month or two ahead of the non-heated reservoirs nearby.

For More Bass, Try Deadly Lures That Are Often Overlooked

Air temperatures in the 50's and southerly breezes should provide the angler an opportunity for some excellent bass fishing, like an experience I had a couple of years ago.

I was shivering in the damp air of a power plant lake, awaiting a surge on the terminal end of my line. The tentative grip of my numb hands on my casting outfit worried me. Deep water winter bass can be cantankerous at times. Locating and catching several largemouth, though, can be worth the agony. My tactical approach follows:

- My cold weather venture began with a review of a topographical map of the water. Through this analysis, I was able to eliminate a lot of water; fishing barren territory seems to be even more of a waste of valuable time in winter weather.

- I first moved to a deep water hump off a submerged creek channel. Noticing a fish on the LCD, I quickly grabbed a rod rigged with a heavy spoon. The bait fell toward the fish and was quickly attacked. Jigging spoons can be that much fun. I never left that hump until I headed for the ramp.

I prefer heavy spoons versus flutter-type spoons, because the former get to the bass quicker and are easier to control. Flutter spoons vibrate, which may, at times, cause the fish to move. They seldom result in a hooked fish on the up-stroke of the rod. The jigging spoon is ideal, though, for the more active, tighter grouped bass normally on the humps.

How To Spoon-Feed Bass Concentrations

Normally, I'll fish the jigging spoon beside the boat in slow "pumps."

- The spoon's action should simulate a wounded shad sinking to the bottom, and then reacting to bounce upward. The lure is allowed to fall to the bottom on a taut line.

- The rod tip should then move upward, bringing the lure up off the bottom no more than two feet. Since there is little vibration on the upsweep of the rod, the spoon's trajectory will be straight and will not veer off to the side.

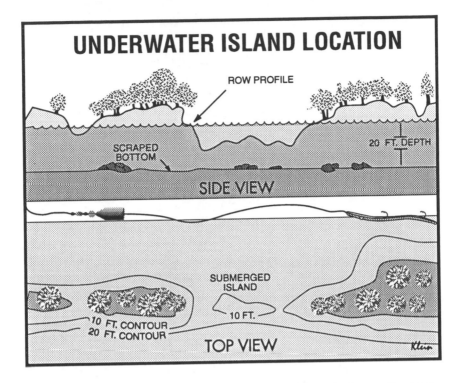

UNDERWATER ISLAND LOCATION

ROW PROFILE

SCRAPED BOTTOM

20 FT. DEPTH

SIDE VIEW

SUBMERGED ISLAND

10 FT. CONTOUR

20 FT. CONTOUR

10 FT.

TOP VIEW

Klein

- In extremely cold waters, the spoons should not be hopped as high off the bottom.

There are two other considerations to effectively hook and fight the fish. Occasionally, a large bass may throw the heavy spoon. As a result, it is critical that all jigging spoons be checked for good, sharp hooks and, if possible, sturdier hooks should be added. Secondly, the reel's drag should also be loosened when fishing relatively open water to insure a better chance of landing big fish.

Other Deep Water Fare May Be The Ticket At Times

When water temperatures are in the 50's or lower, many deep water anglers prefer either a tail spinner lure, scented worm or a jig and eel. The spinner on the tail of a lure, like the Little George, will slow the fall. The colder water requires a slow retrieve too, since the fish are less active.

Plastic worms, such as the Berkley Power Worms, are ideal for fishing slowly in the depths. When Texas-rigged, they are more weedless than just about any other bait presentation...and they catch lots of big fish. Predator and prey metabolism has slowed

Deep water is stable environmentally, and bass often frequent sharp ledges and creek channels in frigid times. They can then move quickly when a norther' hits and secure themselves in deeper depths. A Carolina-rigged worm or jig and eel moved at 6-inch intervals may be the best way to wake up cold bass.

and the best retrieve should probably correspond only to the fish's breathing action.

A jig and eel worked at 6-inch intervals is another excellent way to wake up cold bass. An angler needs to concentrate totally to feel the bait working on the bottom, though, and especially to detect the strike.

- On a retrieve down a hump or dropoff, the free spool button should be punched to allow the lure to "dead fall" to the bottom.

- Over moss-covered bottoms, a 1/4 ounce size jig may be your best bet. I'll opt for a 3/8 ounce version under windy conditions, and go to a 1/2 ounce bait in very deep waters or under very windy conditions.

- In extremely deep waters, a heavily scented plastic trailer or a pork rind eel should be used. Bass normally won't eject them as quickly as they will an unscented trailer.

On my first trip with a stash of jigging spoons, jig and eels, and the conviction to spend substantial time vertically fishing deep water humps, I caught and released a dozen big bass. The cold day was memorable because of the winter, deep-water techniques that I was able to further develop, and because of the nice 7-pound bass that was the prize pulled from the depths.

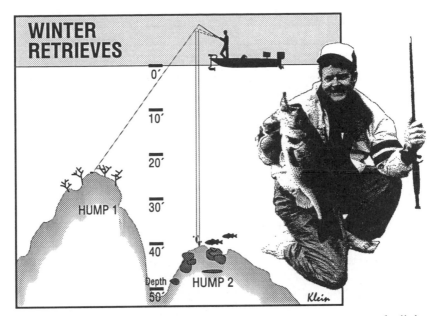

The two most common winter retrieves for deep water structure are the jig 'n eel for depths between 15 and 30 feet and the jiggin' spoon for waters over 30 feet.

On a typical, bitter cold January morning, I launched the boat for a day's chunking on a small power plant lake. The air temperature hovered around freezing and a gusty wind blew at a constant 20 mile-per-hour force. Since learning that day how effective deep water techniques can be, I've taken several huge bass from those types of waters.

The Best Way To Locate Deep Water Bass

Deep water bass haunts aren't difficult to locate. After surveying appropriate maps and selecting waters that may potentially hold big bass, you'll need to get on that water with your most important tool, a chart recorder or LCD. Without the electronics, you may as well be blind; you'll need your "eyes to the bottom."

- Savvy wintertime anglers often use a chart recorder to eliminate water in the deep. For all practical purposes, the recorder is most effective in water deeper than 10 feet, and that's where most pros use them. They want to see fish on the chart paper or LCD before they put a lure down in the depths.

The Deep - Cold Front Escapes   43

- On a strange lake, a good deep water angler may chart practically all day long before putting a bait in the water. Although he may then have only 30 minutes of fishing, it will be extremely productive.

- On a lake that he knows relatively well, 10 minutes of charting may be enough prior to fishing. If fish are not in evidence, the wise angler will check it out quickly and move on.

The jigging spoon can be used for a speedy "check out" and, if productive, the angler may want to back off the deep water structure and drop a jig and eel to a concentration of bass. Fish it slower for more action.

To be a successful cold water angler, you'll need to learn deep water angling techniques. With the right approach to locating bass in the depths, winter productivity should remain high. Frigid weather affects the angler more than it does the concentration of four pound largemouth scattered over that deep water hump!

FRONTAL ATTACKS

Fronts normally have a devastating effect on shallow bass. A northerly wind along with cold night air temperatures can pile up cool waters on the southern shore, making things even tougher for anglers on that side of the lake. Cold winds will affect any exposed shallow waters, regardless of exposure, but a bright sun should start to reheat the leeward shorelines just after the front has passed.

The effects of sunshine and warm southerly winds may even heat protected northern shorelines, and humid winds after a norther' generally turn bass on. At the same time, the southern shore may continue to hold cold water which has been unaffected by the wind. Cold water here will dissipate slower because of the protected shoreline.

The influence of winds, whether from the north or south, play a big part in the water temperature fluctuations. Many of the creeks heavily fished in cold weather run east and west, and the north and south shorelines of these tributaries may vary drastically in temperature. For further information on patterning post-frontal bass, you may want to check out "Bass Patterns - An Angler's Guide" which is book 8 in the BASS SERIES LIBRARY. Ordering details are at the back of this book.

CHAPTER 6

TIPS FOR SOLVING CLEAR WATER PROBLEMS
Clear lake waters and spring-influenced rivers require special techniques

Fish which are unwary in clear water are an exception; the majority are especially cautious. There are ways to increase the number of strikes from the "observers" that swim in those depths, but it is seldom easy. Bass in a visible environment respond to most factors differently than do those living in stained waters.

The typical bass in the visible world of spring runs and clear water lakes is often afraid of any shadow. Their world is under a magnifying glass and they know it. Mistakes or miscalculations are not easily forgiven in clear waters.

Largemouth that venture away from weed or rock-intensive cover are easily spooked by birds flying over clear waters. I once observed a school of small bass that had taken up home at a rock pile just off a long pier behind my condo. Several herons and other water birds would fly low over the water in their approach to light on the low dock. Each time that a large bird's wingspan would block the sun, the bass would scatter from the rock pile.

The clear water environment is usually not as nutrient-rich as stained waters, and the resulting food base is often unique to such bass territories. Crayfish and other crustaceans, as well as smaller versions of the minnow family, are a mainstay in the diet of many clear water bass. In spring-fed tributaries, in particular, stomach content analyses by various states' fisheries biologists have revealed that about 90 percent of the bass' food intake can be crayfish.

Knowing the forage base is one bit of information that can help an angler determine the most appropriate lures or bait. This is explained extensively in the first two volumes of my Bass Series Library. Forage in one clear body of water may differ from that found in others.

- In large, natural lakes with more extensive vegetation growth, the forage may be predominately shiners and sunfish.

- On giant man-made impoundments, the usual prey may be threadfin shad that roam the open, clear waters.

Check Out Water Whose Clarity Varies ... At The Right Time

Some clear waters are high-visibility environments year around, while others clear up only during the cold, low rainfall periods over the winter months. Low waters are often the clearest due to the minimal spring influences then. They can take the form of marsh, ponds, streams, quarries, lakes or reservoirs.

I have a small cabin just off the Santa Fe River in Northern Florida. The water is typically tannic-stained, and although the flowage does have one large spring run and several small springs, cypress trees are the predominant water color influence. Once or twice a year, though, the 27-mile long Santa Fe will become extremely clear.

In the spring, when the nearby Suwannee River is cresting with heavy storm waters, the smaller tributary is, in effect, stopped up. At that time, the Santa Fe's major spring tributary, the Itchetucknee River, pours its crystal clear waters into the flood plain. The result is a much clearer Santa Fe River and fishing it can be tough.

Bass in the Santa Fe are accustomed to stained waters, and any improved clarity is not totally welcomed. Both the largemouth and the rare Suwannee bass feel protected from their predators (fishermen) in waters that are typically stained. In clear waters, they are much more hesitant to move after lures.

How You Can Overcome The Spook Factor

Fortunately, there are effective ways to fish for these bass and to get around the "spook factor" that is usually present. Stealth is an obvious consideration when searching for the clear water bass. Anyone who has tossed flies into a 10-foot wide brook or a 20-foot diameter beaver pond for trout should know what I'm talking

Larry Larsen on Bass Tactics

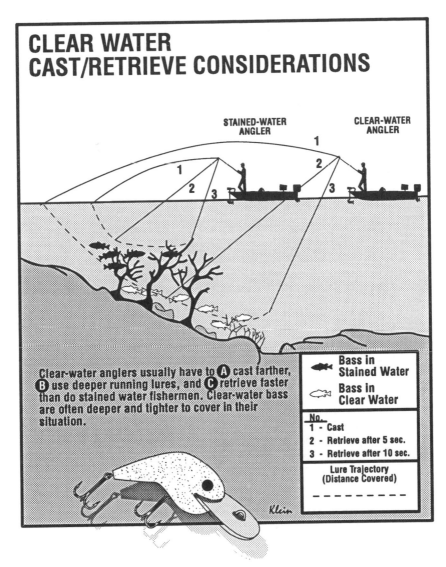

CLEAR WATER
CAST/RETRIEVE CONSIDERATIONS

STAINED-WATER
ANGLER

CLEAR-WATER
ANGLER

Clear-water anglers usually have to **A** cast farther, **B** use deeper running lures, and **C** retrieve faster than do stained water fishermen. Clear-water bass are often deeper and tighter to cover in their situation.

Bass in
Stained Water

Bass in
Clear Water

No.
1 - Cast
2 - Retrieve after 5 sec.
3 - Retrieve after 10 sec.

Lure Trajectory
(Distance Covered)

about. Many bass anglers, however, haven't been exposed to ultra-wary, small-water fish.

- The careful, quiet approach is usually most productive when fishing for clear water bass, especially those in small spring runs.

- Bank anglers should be aware of the vibrations their feet carry through the usually firm soil when trampling through shoreline rocks and trees. Movements should be slow and deliberate.

- Plan your movements and walk softly to take advantage of the shoreside cover for camouflage.

The best area to learn shoreline "stealth" is probably on a trout stream. I was 10 years old when I first waded and stumbled down a Colorado mountain stream. I quickly learned to park myself behind a tree trunk, rock or tall bush before casting to the great looking spot on the opposite shoreline. Stealth may also incorporate camouflage:

- Wearing camouflage clothing along a shoreline will help you blend into the environment.

- If angling from a boat, clothing with shades of blue or gray will blend in with the sky or the surroundings. Bass can easily see bright colors that stand out from the background.

Blend Into The Shadows For A Successful Dark Approach

The guise of the limited light is a key to many anglers' productivity on super clear waters. Mistakes made by the fishermen are not easily detected by the bass. The angler can often fool many more largemouth on clear waters after the sun sets. When darkness moves in, usually the bass' inhibitions about moving around and striking lures are fewer.

I've taken many daytime largemouth from those lakes and other similar ones, but for maximum success, I will fish them during the hours of low-light levels. Here's how I analyze that, to catch more and bigger bass:

- In such waters, light usually causes the clear-water fish to move tighter to various types of habitat.

- To be productive during a high-sun period, I commonly rely on lures and baits that can be fished tighter to the cover and/or deeper.

Clear water bass on Table Rock often hold in the depths nearer to a log or boulder while those in East Lake "Toho" bury themselves in a dense vegetation. Bass on other clear waters likewise seek out the shadows and protection of cover.

Remote Finds Offer Less Wary Fish

Discover a clear water stream or pond that receives little or no fishing pressure and you can have a real ball. Bass in such waters are great fun to catch and watch as they go head-to-head with you.

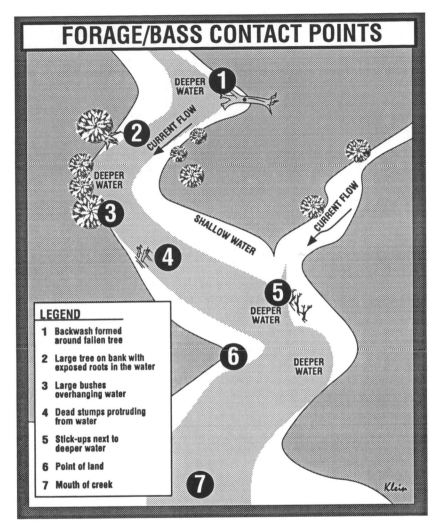

FORAGE/BASS CONTACT POINTS

DEEPER WATER

CURRENT FLOW

DEEPER WATER

SHALLOW WATER

CURRENT FLOW

DEEPER WATER

DEEPER WATER

LEGEND

1 Backwash formed around fallen tree

2 Large tree on bank with exposed roots in the water

3 Large bushes overhanging water

4 Dead stumps protruding from water

5 Stick-ups next to deeper water

6 Point of land

7 Mouth of creek

Klein

Whether in a lake or stream, clear water bass usually jump easily through the air/water interface. It's as though the boundary of their environment and ours is difficult for the largemouth to detect.

In such an environment, the angler is as visible to the bass as the bass is to the angler. I once found a remote little spring-fed creek where the largemouth bravely followed my bounding plastic worm out from shoreline cover with seemingly reckless abandon.

Tips For Solving Clear Water Problems   49

I watched them time and time again, as they gulped my current-swept fare and quickly turned to depart. With such advance warning, it was hardly surprising that my hook set was true. The battle ensued, both on top and below the surface, and all was viewed as though water and air were one.

That small waterway was crystal-clear, the largemouth bass were numerous and hungry, and fortunately, they were "virgin" fish, having seldom seen a fisherman. Although I caught and released 16 pugnacious bass that afternoon, such clear water locations are admittedly rare.

A six-pounder that sucked in my pumpkinseed worm probably had never been on the terminal end of tackle before. Its aerial display was a show I won't soon forget, and for once, I didn't have to watch for the line to move toward the surface in order to predict the glorious jump.

Obviously, that action in the remote waters was something that many anglers may have difficulty finding. Bass in that small, winding spring run were difficult to reach from the larger tributary below. Fishing pressure there was very minimal and in fact, very few stream anglers even know about the run. Places like that do exist, and they are quite a discovery!

CHAPTER 7

HOW TO TACKLE
CLEAR WATER BASS

Getting a lure to them and a line on them may be easy

The reality is that it's usually difficult to catch clear-water bass in any water when fishing too close. For most situations, and naturally for deeper bass, long casts are important.

A long rod with the capability of tossing a lightweight lure several yards is a valuable tool in this environment. I consider my Berkley B50-7MH to be the ultimate in long rods. The seven-foot graphite casting rod can accurately heave a lightweight lure a great distance.

Line size is also important in a transparent environment where each predator looks ever so closely at the prey before attacking. Lighter line is an effective way to entice more strikes. The smaller diameter makes it more difficult for the bass to detect, and the finer "thread" also allows the lures to exhibit maximum action. Less line resistance means deeper running crankbaits as well.

- When determining the size of line to employ in clear waters, the habitat being fished is a vital consideration. In highly-vegetated areas, 10-pound test monofilament may be as light as one dare go, while on a deep, cover-barren reservoir, the choice may be six- or even four-pound test for best action.

Strike Detection Is Not Always Easy In Clear Waters

Many anglers have difficulty in detecting a deep-water strike. If you have ever been underwater observing bass as they strike crankbaits, you've probably noticed that in many instances, the

How To Tackle Clear Water Bass   51

angler did not even know that a bass had inhaled and spit out the lure.

Such a difficulty in detecting strikes is particularly true when fishing a slow bait, like grub or worm. Three things will help your hook-up ratio:

1. One way to aid in detection is to use a graphite rod which has the blank extending all the way through the butt for maximum transferal of any vibration.

2. Another way to detect more strikes is to closely watch the line for any unusual movement.

3. Yet another way to help detect some of the deep strikes is to place your index finger on the line in front of the spool.

Using the above, you may be able to detect the softest of strikes. You'll still miss some, but your deep-water catch rate should improve.

Water Body	Primary Habitat	Line (clear)	Lure	
			Type	Color
Small Spring Runs	Rock, sand	6-8#	small spinner, grub, plug	silver, white crayfish-hued
Large Rivers	Rock, logs	8-10#	crankbait, jig, crayfish replica	crayfish, brown red, white
Reservoirs	Rock, some trees	8-10#	top water plug, crankbait, jig	clear, white shad-hued
Natural Lakes	Dense vegetation	10-12#	worm, snake live bait	motor oil, brown multi-color

TACKLE CONSIDERATIONS FOR CLEAR WATERS

The Best Lures For Clear Water

What do clear water bass most often want? Waters with low-nutrient levels and a smaller size prey dictate smaller lures for the productive fisherman. Brown and red combinations, as well as green hues, are natural colors in that highly visible world. Silver and white minnow imitations are attractive lures to the largemouth on clear waters.

Spinnerbaits, in-line spinners and spoons that directly resemble the action of common prey in the water's forage base are

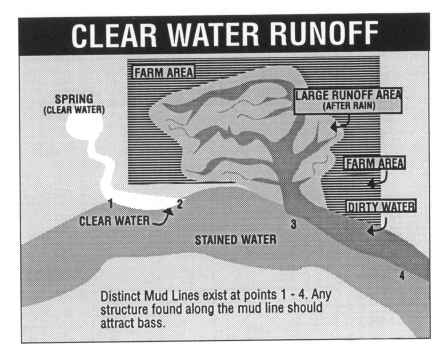

CLEAR WATER RUNOFF

FARM AREA

SPRING
(CLEAR WATER)

LARGE RUNOFF AREA
(AFTER RAIN)

FARM AREA

DIRTY WATER

1   2
CLEAR WATER

3

STAINED WATER

4

Distinct Mud Lines exist at points 1 - 4. Any structure found along the mud line should attract bass.

productive. Any crankbait or plastic lure resembling a crayfish is likewise a good choice.

- Key in on the forage of the clear water environment before you select the lure.

- If bass in a clear water environment appear aggressive, use a rapid retrieve and active bait.

Lures that can be retrieved faster in such waters will often trigger impulse strikes. For example, a tandem spinnerbait that "bulges" the surface on the retrieve will draw action from a large-mouth several feet away. Chartreuse and white skirts seem to be productive colors for spinnerbaits.

Check Out The Live Bait Possibilities

In cooler waters, live bait may be the right lure to fool a wary largemouth. Bait in a cold water situation are sluggish, and a minimal of activity may entice the bass then.

- When clear water bass won't move far for an artificial lure, they will strike at a live bait.

▄EMPLOY THE BASICS FOR CLEAR WATER BASS▄

Downsizing lines and lures, faster retrieves, angling in low-light levels, "sneaking" up on the fish, selecting baits that closely imitate the predominant forage and fishing deeper and tighter to cover are only "guidelines" for clear-water bass success. I've discovered several productive ploys for specific clear waters over the years.

- In small spring-run tributaries, cast small spinners, injured-minnow plugs, rubber crayfish imitations, and 4- and 6-inch worms.

- In larger, clear rivers, cast natural-looking bait replicas such as crayfish crankbaits, jigs, and rubber eels, lizards, and crayfish for more than your share of largemouth.

- Bass that call a large clear-water reservoir home favor shad-hued crankbaits and jig and eels.

- In weedy and clear, natural lakes, try tossing plastic worms and snakes, rigged in a swimming or bottom-hugging manner, or live bait such as crayfish or shiners.

Clear water situations don't have to be frustrating. Just because you can see the bottom at 20 feet is no reason to become disgusted and move to other waters. While waters of great clarity may be reluctant to give up their bounty, they do.

- During the spawn, some "slow motion" live bait activity may be needed to garner a strike.

In high-visibility environments, success sometimes dictates going with the real thing. Again, knowing the predominant forage will direct the choice of bait. Shad, not often available commercially, salamanders in the spring, shiners and crayfish are popular with both anglers and clear water largemouth.

Try The Toned-Down Offerings For More Bass

Lightweight tackle, thin line and a tiny minnow plug may produce best. Most anglers who have spent time on the water have noticed a slow, weak baitfish that appears to be in failing health. I've seen clear-water bass explode on crippled shad that lay quivering on the surface. Slow moving baits that simulate the action work well, but they have to be realistic in appearance. Bass have ample time to examine them.

- Toned-down offerings such as clear plastic top water plugs and buzz and spinnerbaits with clear plastic blades seem to produce more bass on the clear waters of large reservoirs than they do in others.

- The big top water bait, even in a clear finish, usually draws fish from a long way off.

- Pulsating baits, such as plastic or pork-tipped jigs, when crawled across the bottom, can also be effective.

Another unique approach to clear water problems is the one-two punch of a top water plug, like the Zara Spook, and a second rod rigged with a plastic grub or worm. When used in deep, clear waters, the combination is tough to beat.

Wary bass won't always come to the surface to hit the larger Zara, but they might swirl at it giving themselves away.

I've often found that tossing a red, blue or shad-colored grub or small six-inch worm back to the site of the swirl will have exciting results. The bass that would just swirl at the top water plug will often suck in a weighted grub or worm bouncing below the plug.

CHAPTER 8

TINY WATERS
TINY CRAFT

Tactics for locating bass in small waters

For great bass angling, mini water offerings are hard to top. Fishing them can be a peaceful experience where one can find a type of solitude not common on bigger lakes that stretch for miles. The enjoyment of getting back to the basics can also be a thrill for many anglers who have become too caught up in the maze of competitive, high-performance fishing found in some circles today.

Fishing small waters can be unencumbered by sophistication. Sure, the angler can still use his Color-C-Lector and depth finders, but his approach and what he is able to develop in his own mind is usually the prime ingredient to success on smaller bodies of water. The very best fishing trips are often enhanced by the beautiful surroundings, and these waters generally offer much scenery in addition to productivity.

Finding good, small waters is relatively easy. When the topo map reveals difficult access, that usually means minimal fishing pressure. Pick up your little boat and try out the bass fishing. Tiny waters and small craft go together, and you will seldom forget the bass opportunities.

The productive small water angler must pay close attention to the little environment. Stealth is usually vital to the success of a venture into tiny waters. A bass raised in that environment is very cognizant of what is happening around him. If cattle drink out of a two-acre pond, the bass know it. If a blue heron moves along the shallows of a marsh, bass will be aware of its presence.

Small waters can offer a productive fishery away from the high-speed crowds that frequent larger bodies of water. With a smaller forage base, many small ponds offer bass of smaller proportions. But often, there are many available in the one to three-pound range.

The noisy presence of alligators, otters and other large "creatures" including man, may "strike fear into a bass' heart." Seldom then will the bass strike at the angler's lure. The cautious angler who moves his small craft with minimal noise or disturbance to the delicate ecosystem is the one who will catch more fish. Tiny water bass prefer peace and quiet.

Barely Navigable Waters Offer Overlooked Bass

I have often explored new waters with a variety of small craft over the years. I have reached deeper, wider pools full of eager bass by lifting some boats over obstacles in shallow water.

One spring-fed run that I fished averaged one foot deep. The five-foot depths every hundred yards or so held bass, and some good ones.

I enjoy finding such concentrations of largemouth pinpointed like that. I fished seven such pools, each for five minutes or five bass, whichever came first. Thirty bass were caught and released, including a 5 1/2 pounder. Navigation between the pools took time, some 15 to 20 minutes each, but it was worth it.

Many waters like that are often are inaccessible to the big bass boat crowd. Such overlooked waters require hard work just to get

WHERE TO LOOK FOR BASS IN PONDS

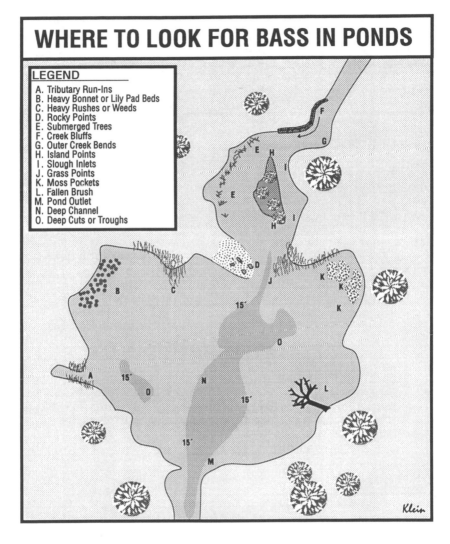

LEGEND
A. Tributary Run-Ins
B. Heavy Bonnet or Lily Pad Beds
C. Heavy Rushes or Weeds
D. Rocky Points
E. Submerged Trees
F. Creek Bluffs
G. Outer Creek Bends
H. Island Points
I. Slough Inlets
J. Grass Points
K. Moss Pockets
L. Fallen Brush
M. Pond Outlet
N. Deep Channel
O. Deep Cuts or Troughs

a crack at the fish. Some guidelines to maximize the catch should be kept in mind:

- Small craft usually enable an angler to take a more quiet, productive approach.

- Shorter casts, which are usually more accurate than longer ones, are more appropriate on tiny waters.

- Accuracy is most important on small waters where shallow habitat is predominant.

The mistakes of the caster are more exposed on small water hideouts. Strikers are easier to hook, though, and the fish easier to battle on a short line. For further information on fishing shallows, you may want to check out "Shallow Water Bass" which is book 5 in the BASS SERIES LIBRARY. Ordering details are found at the back of this book.

Look Past The Entrance Sandbar To The Bounty Beyond

Concentrations of bass in tiny waters like canals are easier to work from a closer position. Canal areas are well known for their enticement to bedding bass. Many, such as one I fished a while back, have a very shallow sandbar at their entrance, which limits boat and angling activity. The canals typically deepen once past the entrance "blockage."

I had to get out of my small boat and carry it over the sand bar. The water was ankle deep over the canal's first 20 yards, and then the depth dropped to five feet. How the numerous largemouth bass between four and seven pounds got there, I don't know, but five of them caught and released provided me an enjoyable afternoon.

Know Where The Bass May Be Moving Or Holding

Spring angling on tiny waters can be fantastic. Bass often move to the far reaches of such waters in an effort to get away from any potential disturbances to their spawning tasks. Tiny ponds, marshes and narrow creeks are often topographically limited to angling from small boats.

Marsh, swamp and prairie potholes are typical of natural lowland waters that are difficult to access. Small rigs can be poled or pulled through extremely shallow spots to reach deeper, more productive water.

Moving water places can be the best spots to find bass in small waters. Forage fish are more accessible there to the predator bass. Certain keys to finding them should be understood.

- Marsh or swamp waters that drain into deeper, small water holes make the latter very productive. Bait fish and other medium-sized forage frequent these areas to enjoy food, plankton and other minute organisms. Weaker specimens are swept out of the extremely shallow areas into the deeper holes during runoff situations.

- Rainfall, huge irrigation pumps, locks or other intermittent causes of the flow movement have a great effect on the feeding of lowland bass. The angler who can take advantage of a drain flow situation, whether it's runoff or a pull (suction of water), will often find exceptional largemouth angling.

Check Out The Other Tiny Hotspots

Remote areas that receive very little fishing pressure often have deep holes, and while some may be difficult to find, many arc not. Huge cypress trees in a circular pattern usually denote the presence of deeper water. Other changes from marsh grass to trees or various types of vegetation may reveal deeper waters. Too, deeper spots are the ones that hold water year around and provide largemouth the opportunity to flourish.

Potholes, isolated in a sea of submerged grass, can be hotspots, and a narrow, square stern canoe is ideal for such places. A rear-mounted outboard is often necessary to power through vegetation to reach the bass holes. Move silently into these potholes, though, for maximum action.

Cut the engine some 15 yards away and either pole or paddle through the vegetation around the hole. Then, cast into the weed edges, but don't neglect the center of a small pothole. That should result in some bass.

Larry Larsen on Bass Tactics

CHAPTER 9
MINI-WATER LURES AND PRESENTATIONS
How to select your arsenal and position the boat

When fishing tiny waters, a smart angler will often modify the complexion of his tackle box. The exact look should depend on the water being fished.

Worms, such as Berkley's scented Power Worms, are very productive when fished slow in tiny, weedy environments. Near-surface plugs, like the Bomber Long A, are especially successful when tossed near the weedy perimeter of these holes. The quiet angling with the "twitching" plug will often have a chance at the biggest fish in the hole.

Isolated canals, borrow pits, farm ponds and stock tanks all offer the small boat angler an opportunity to catch some bass. With the limited access to these waters, many fishermen go elsewhere. These places are even scoffed at due to their size, yet many can produce bigger bass than the much larger lakes nearby. Look at the state records and you'll often find "private pond" listed.

Small ponds hold big fish that seldom are pressured by masses of anglers. Ironically, such waters may possess a smaller forage-base size and our lure selection might have to take that into account. You may have to scale down the length or girth of a plug, for example, to reap the best results.

I've always believed in "big baits for big bass" and I still follow that philosophy, but prior to any lure selection, you should consider the fishery composition and size of predominant forage. That's the theme driven home in my two volumes of "Follow The Forage For Better Bass Angling."

Don't Overlook What Every Other Angler Does

I like to fish small, ugly waters due to lack of angling pressure on such bodies. I've often found hungry fish and, if I were keeping them, a quick limit. Even with my 4-wheel drive vehicle, I come across numerous waters each year where I can't launch my 18-foot bass boat. Here are some of the better places that I will always check out:

- Canals that lead "nowhere" are small fisheries with limited forage growth, yet they harbor some great bass fishing. Depths usually vary from a couple of feet to seven or eight. Many hold bass while others do not. Those with minimal water circulation may become stagnant and offer few sport fish.

- Borrow pits are dug beside roadways to gather fill dirt for road construction, and most get stocked naturally. Many yield bass, but most are overlooked. These waters can look ugly, yet be full of largemouth.

Select The Right Craft For The Particular Waters

Small craft in most tiny waters are very effective. Pointed or square-stern canoes are obviously suited for tight places, but if creek banks wind much, or there are more than a few trees to move past, boat length becomes a critical factor. My small water craft is a small, one-man kayak-type boat that is very stable.

Little six- and eight-foot-long glass boats are sometimes ideal for sharp turns involved in maneuvering through a flooded forest at the back of a cove, or up a winding creek channel. The back of coves and the upper reaches of small creeks that freshen up rivers are often inaccessible to wide, deep draft boats.

You'll probably need a small, two man boat for these tiny waters. Such craft are more suitable for the tiny waters anyway. They were designed with such wet environments in mind, and fishing from a small craft on these waters is usually more productive than from a larger, seemingly more comfortable rig. Canoes, little two-man boats and small aluminum john boats enable the small water angler to move about quietly, yet efficiently.

Boat Positioning Is A Key To Catching Small Water Bass

Sculling a small craft is an extremely silent way to propel it. The sculling angler can often fish with his free hand while guiding the boat. This type paddling is a one-handed operation, and the paddle is never lifted from the water. The blade edge is moved forward and then turned 90 degrees and brought back with flat side

The habitat varies along housing developments, but the bass are usually content with whatever is provided. Access to tiny waters from a small boat is possible.

forward and then turned 90 degrees and brought back with flat side moving against the water to propel the boat forward. The stroke with a short paddle becomes easy with practice.

Trolling slowly or drifting with maneuvering corrections are relatively easy. Without the paddle slapping the surface of the water, this method of motion is also quieter than a trolling motor. The intermittent running of an electric motor can sometimes be distracting to a feeding fish.

How To Check Out Offshore Areas

When moving about a small water in my small boat, I'll check out any existing changes in depths. I'll fish any shoreline habitat or offshore cover with a selection of crankbaits or plastic worms. This often requires some investigation and hard work. Two other things may help to isolate the better structure:

1. A pH meter

2. Portable depth finder

Deep diving crankbaits are adequate for doing evaluations of the bottom terrain, if you don't have a flasher or LCD.

The offshore structure of many farm ponds, stock tanks, etc. has been a part of my fishing life since boyhood. In fact, a seven-pound Kansas largemouth from the deepest timbered-spot in my

Many other small impoundments have produced similar size fish, and I have a special place in my memory for such pond activities.

Approach The Pond From The Deep

I usually start my angling adventure in the deepest water available in such a pond. I'll cast to the heaviest cover, and often, this will be submerged trees. They are magnets to pond bass. Heavy submerged wood structure invites numerous snakes, worms and other skinny food for bass. Plastic worms are, thus, my favorite in such surroundings. Here's my scenario:

1. I'll cast these to the heaviest stickups around and worry about getting the bass out after he strikes the lure. Concentration and casting accuracy are where the mind should be.

2. Once the deep, heavy cover areas have been worked thoroughly, I'll move into shallower confines, such as the creeks or ditches that may feed the small impoundments.

3. Then, I'll check out the coves that often harbor flooded brush or aquatic weed beds. I'll move the boat slowly through these areas and fish them patiently for best results.

There is no need to hurry when fishing the tiny waters. Competition for the likely-looking holes is usually non-existent, and that makes it easier on all of us!

CHAPTER 10

LIGHTWEIGHT FINESSE
When and where light tackle catches more big fish

Lightweight tackle means extra fun to many anglers, but its use also requires one to use a little more finesse for big fish. Laying down the Texas-rigged worm outfit with 20-pound test line and picking up a light spinning outfit is difficult for some die-hard bass casters. Doing so, though, could pay dividends.

A friend and I had been searching three hours for largemouths with very little success. Two small bass were the result of our "hawg-hunting." The hot June sun was beginning to bead sweat on our foreheads as we picked up our spinning rigs and began to plug for any size bass with lightweight lures.

My partner's second cast with a small Rebel to a few submerged trees was retrieved three feet before the lure stopped and he set back hard. The huge bass leaped a foot above the lake's surface, spraying water everywhere. The light rod was bent double as my friend exerted pressure to carefully work her toward the surface.

He strained at the rod working the fish free from a submerged tree trunk which it had tried to swim around. That area of the small lake was full of submerged brush and flooded trees, which always pose a potential problem during any battle with a respected foe. The lunker again leaped, clearing the surface and headed for deeper, open water, much to our relief.

The small, jointed plug still had a firm grasp of its predator's lower jaw when I slid the net in front of her. The bass was truly a monster. Her sides were thick and powerful. This fish made the 12-pounder that I had caught on the previous trip seem small, and it did so without displaying a fat gut, which is typical of many bass over 10 pounds.

The fish caught on the light outfit and injured minnow lure was weighed six hours later on state-inspected scales and registered at 15 pounds and 2 ounces. As that experience proved, light rods and reels in shallow areas are not just a small fish experience. Some real wallhangers can be caught.

Why You Should Fish Lightweight Outfits

More veteran anglers are turning to the thrills of lightweight tackle each day, and they're finding that their bass catches have increased substantially. Ten years ago, few used light tackle. Most tackle companies today though offer popular, high-quality lightweight rigs.

The lighter line capabilities and easier handling have aided the lightweight tackle fisherman in producing more bass. Shallow lakes and ponds throughout the country are what most anglers with the lightweight tackle prefer to fish, since they feel most comfortable in such surroundings.

How To Analyze The Right Habitat

Many natural lake bottoms abound with sink holes, rock outcroppings, springs, fallen trees and creek beds. All of this can be found in shallow water and most is accessible to the light tackle angler.

Probably the most important thing a light tackle fisherman can do is learn to read shallow water and establish a pattern. Many keys to bottom structure exist for the careful observer. Since structure provides food and comfort to a bass, understanding how to recognize this structure is important.

A common fishing problem on natural waters is that there is just too much "fishy" looking water. It is hard to concentrate on finding lake bottom structure when the eye is full of beautiful cypress trees loaded with Spanish moss flitting in the breeze, and a field of pads between the trees and your boat. Looking past all that can help you home in on the best spots to finesse a bass. Finding the best could require some extensive investigation.

- Look over shallow water habitat for distinct points.

- If the lake is shallow and the land surrounding it is fairly flat, the points are not as noticeable as on a deeper lake.

- There is always a point where a tributary or creek bed enters or leaves the lake. This may be in the back of a cove.

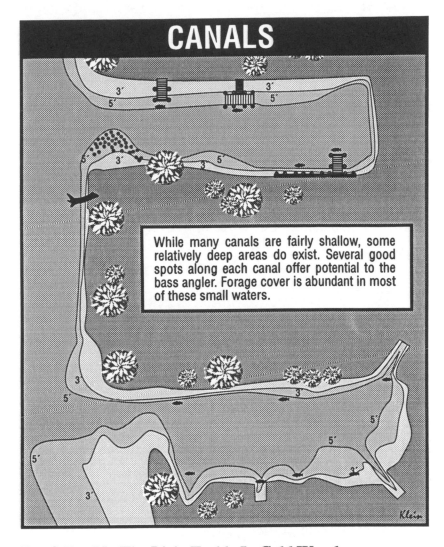

CANALS

While many canals are fairly shallow, some relatively deep areas do exist. Several good spots along each canal offer potential to the bass angler. Forage cover is abundant in most of these small waters.

Don't Put Up The Light Tackle In Cold Weather

Light tackle performs any time of the year. On one extremely cold day several years ago, the air temperature had fallen from the upper 40's to mid 30's as a "norther" blew in. The wind steadily shoved 30 mph winds at the boat, and gusts to 45 mph literally froze our guides closed.

Several boats were fishing that day, but most had to spend an hour or two tied up to a small, but warm fish camp on the west shore. I was able to coax three 14-inch bass out of the white caps on the windward shore and no one else had taken a largemouth after six hours.

One angler did, however, pull in a keeper. He went to his live well and pulled out his single fish, a 10-pound, 5-ounce lunker. While everyone else was tossing heavy baits, he had been flipping a small floating minnow plug in a quiet cove. His light tackle with 8-pound test was the ticket.

How To Fish Pockets And Potholes With Tiny Fare

Another area where lightweight tackle is especially productive is one with small pockets and potholes lying in heavy cover such as grass, bulrushes or lily pads. These areas can be a utopia in a shallow lake and should be explored thoroughly. Bass use these for protection and ambush. The scattered light in these areas is what all fish prefer.

Why do small lures work so well in such places? One of the reasons is size.

• The small lures can be tossed into tiny pockets without creating too big a disturbance.

• Too much commotion in a small pothole can frighten away all nearby fish.

• Most lures are too heavy or bulky to effectively fish these areas.

Shallow lakes are by nature weedy, and generally have some sort of weedline. The points should be worked before any other portion of the weeds. After that, the angler should forget working the entire weedline and just look at the shore. Many times the shoreline of a shallow lake can give a good indication of a good area to search, while the weeds in the lake may all look alike. The bass may be in one of two places:

1. In the spring, the bass will be back inside the weedline.

2. After spawning, the bass typically move to the weedline nearest a dropoff and set up home for the summer.

The entire weedline should be checked for a dropoff. Weedlines don't just happen! There has to be a reason for the weeds not to propagate beyond a certain point. Usually, it's because the depth limits light penetration. This is exactly what our eyelid-less quarry seek!

The Best Finesse Knot Is The Palomar.

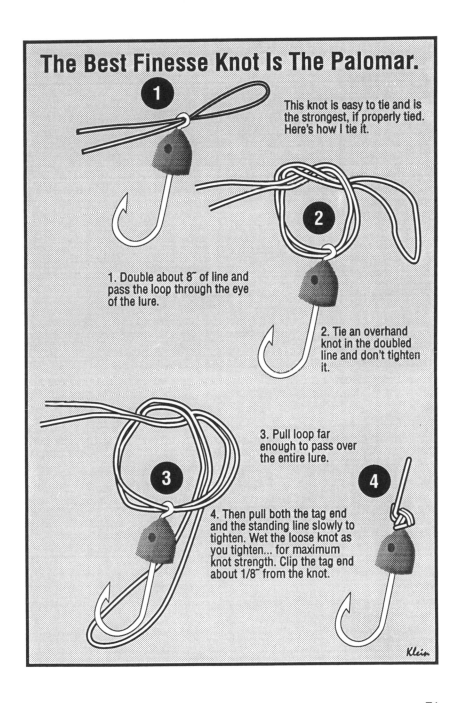

This knot is easy to tie and is the strongest, if properly tied. Here's how I tie it.

1. Double about 8" of line and pass the loop through the eye of the lure.

2. Tie an overhand knot in the doubled line and don't tighten it.

3. Pull loop far enough to pass over the entire lure.

4. Then pull both the tag end and the standing line slowly to tighten. Wet the loose knot as you tighten... for maximum knot strength. Clip the tag end about 1/8" from the knot.

Klein

FINESSE TACKLE THOUGHTS

Casting lightweight lures can sometimes pose problems to the baitcaster more accustomed to 25-pound test line. Ultralight spinning rods and reels are great for pursuing bass in thin and somewhat contained waters, such as canal banks. Lines testing 6- to 8-pound test and lures of 1/32 to 1/8 ounce are preferred tackle in many areas.

Shallow water bass will sometimes spook easily and a soft landing, slow moving morsel is the angler's best bet for success. Lightweight lures that are tops on most anglers' lists are the following:

1. Small floating minnow plugs

2. Mini-vibrating baits

3. Tiny crankbaits

4. Small worms, slugs, grubs and hollow tubes

5. Tiny spinners and spinnerbaits

A four-inch Berkley Power Slug is a favorite bait of mine for tossing into small waters. Under most conditions, a near-surface worm in a pumpkinseed hue is hard to top.

I've noticed that large fish sometimes will not travel far to chase a fast lure, but will glide out from their hangout and take a slowly presented lure. At other times, the small, but fast crankbaits trigger strikes not possible in other ways.

Small lures and lightweight tackle can be powerful producers in various places under many different circumstances. A smaller food cycle generally predominates in shallow water and smaller water bodies, and thus, smaller lures are more productive than the larger ones.

Check Out The Tight Places

Everyone who has fished a variety of lakes has probably noticed and fished at least one canal. Many waters around the country have canals, but the trick here is to scan their length, particularly where they enter the lake or river. Here are some spots to check out:

- Canal Mouths - Most canals are dug at an even depth, and seldom is that the same as the depth of the lake it enters. Thus, a 5- to 10-foot drop is often found at the point where the canal digging ended. Most of the time, this is a good bass habitat for tossing light lures.

- Canal Intersections - Many times canals cross each other and a depth search may locate a five- to 17-foot instant drop, such as one I found just off Lake Poinsett (central Florida) in a residential area of canals feeding the lake.

Boat trails exist in many shallow grassy lakes and may also provide a drop of two to three feet.

Check Out These Lightweight Tackle Spots In Rivers

Rivers often have numerous shallow canals which offer good finesse fishing opportunities on structure at their mouths. The river depths vary, but generally they range from 10 to 20 feet. Many times, "holes" have been dug deeper than the lake or canal in order to obtain a good start on fill for dikes.

Some of the keys to selecting the best spot to toss a small plug or worm rig are relatively obvious.

- Locate structure in shallow river on the outer bends. The outer bends are generally the deepest part of a river and contain bottom structure, such as sunken trees or rocks.

- Fish any point which is defined at the intersection of another tributary or canal entrance. This is where the greatest topographical change may occur. It offers potential holding structure for large-mouth.

For the light tackle man, isolated structure on a river is less hazardous when a bass is hooked. Often the fish will swim away from the entanglement. Light line and tackle is most appropriate in such areas. A little stealth, quality tackle and correct lure presentation is all that's required for a lot of fun.

Larry Larsen on Bass Tactics

CHAPTER 11

SUBURB BASSING
How to check out urban bass opportunities

The 12-foot alligator that swam in the 1/2-mile long canal looked menacing, but we usually shared the water with no incident. The waterway was surrounded by residential development, manicured lawns and a concrete bulkhead, but it was still where the alligator called home. I called it one of the state's best bass holes.

That favorite warm-weather spot of mine was in a home development where I lived for three years back in the '70s. I've since visited (and lived on) several small suburb lakes and canals around the country, and most hold bass. The alligator that called those waters "home" was a common sight along the canal and was more partial to duck dinner. He left me to chasing largemouth of impressive numbers and size.

On many summer afternoons, I would grab a handful of worms after work and drag my lightweight polystyrene boat a quarter of a block to the water. The 10-fish limit (existing at that time) of two-to four-pound bass from the home-rimmed canal took around four hours, and all were released. Big fish existed, but I never caught one to beat out the canal's top bass which was taken by a young boy. It was just a couple of ounces shy of the 14-pound mark. Several largemouth exceeding eight pounds were caught, however.

Many of the best bass waters in the country are not those large reservoirs that attract big-money tournaments and publicity. They are the small, suburb waters that are sprinkled around golf courses, country clubs and housing developments. While some of the lakes and canals are off-limits to the public, many are open to all. The vast majority are overlooked by the bass boat crowd, so that leaves the bass bounty to just a few.

Residential Development and Golf Course Ponds

Deeper Water

A look at a typical layout of a waterway which meanders through a residential development and along country club fairways and greens may help an angler focus on some of the more productive areas. Golfers try to stay out of the water, but fishermen will want to be in it at the right spot. The locations in the figure are a good place to start.

1. **RUN-OUTS** - *Any new water source from the lakes above will often attract baitfish and, in turn, bass. These areas can be great after a rainshower. In spring-fed waters, the flow can be continuous and so can the action. These are multiple fish "holes" and a limit can often be taken from such a sport.*

2. **BRIDGES** - *Catwalks or man-made bridges over narrow waterways can be very productive. Shade and cover are present and deep water usually exists beneath such structures. Most waterways have some form of crossing over them and they are often real fish magnets. The least traveled overcrossings should be tried first.*

3. **BORROW HOLES** - *The water hazards near elevated greens are where these deeper holes usually exist. The earth for raising greens and berms usually comes from nearby, and a lake offers an excellent source for the fill. Bass hold on such spots but it may take some casting with a deep-running lure or heavy weighted worm to find the hole.*

4. **ISOLATED WATER** - *The small, remote waters may provide the best opportunity if traffic or fishing pressure is a problem. Surprises often await the fisherman who casts the tiny potholes.*

5. **DEEP SHORELINE** - *The deeper water near a shore rich in aquatic vegetation can be bass fishing glory. And, it can be difficult to find! Abrupt endings to rushes, weed mats or grass can tip off the presence of the deeper water swinging in close to shore.*

6. **DEEP SINKS** - *The drop-offs in the middle of a lake or canal can only be found by fishing the area with sinking lures (or with a depth finder if a small boat is used). Larger bass move to such areas for reduced light penetration and better thermal conditions.*

7. **OVERHANGS** - *The man-made structures which project out over a body of water create excellent cover for our quarry. Shade and depth are generally present along with the bass.*

8. **SHORT NECKS** - *Waterway canals or lakes that neck down for short runs are perfect ambush points for bass. Current flow and/or depth may increase the desirability for largemouth and the successful angler won't be far away.*

9. **FINGER COVES** - *Irregular shorelines generally feature little coves or "pockets." Bass in an active feeding mood seeking protection from the early or late sun often turn to places like this. For best results, approach these small coves quietly.*

How To Gain Access To These Overlooked Waters

Access to these tiny waters from a bank or small boat is possible. Manicured waterways with largemouth bass can be found around many residential and business developments. They provide small esthetic lakes that contain superb angling opportunities. Residential developments often offer the amenities of nicely landscaped waterways, many of which are loaded with bass that have little exposure to man.

Golf courses in many urban areas have great bass waters hiding under the guise of water hazards. In the old days, that's all they were, but today, many country club managers and golf course architects are giving careful consideration to the bass fishery in the water hazards. There are two reasons for the improved bass fishing in such places.

1. Fishery management techniques, such as forage enhancement, stocking programs and water level manipulation, are often in place on country club waters.

2. Often, club managers fertilize their waters each year, and that generates good plankton growth in the lakes, which is essential for high bass productivity.

Suburb waterways often have sand bottoms, adequate aquatic vegetation and are stocked with a good staple of sport fish, including largemouth bass. Such waters may be in a variety of configurations:

- natural ponds
- sloughs and marshes
- man-made lakes
- spring-fed canals
- sand pit lakes
- creeks and rivers
- oxbow lakes and bayous

Developments spring up around such places, and public access may be possible at their shoreline.

Permission to fish can often be obtained from a homeowner, apartment manager or caretaker. Golf courses are sometimes closed down for a day each week, offering a chance for anglers to obtain approval to fish the water hazards. Cooler months in the north can be slow and, again, permission can be obtained.

Where You Should Look For Development Largemouth

Good bass structure may be difficult to find on development waters. The wise angler, though, should try to develop a mental picture of the topography. Bass in the suburbs are no different than those in large lakes; they congregate in areas that provide food and cover. Fishing below the 13th green (after golf course hours) or beside a new patio home may take some getting used to, but the best tactics to use are similar to those that are productive elsewhere.

Establishing a productive pattern is vital to catching largemouth, and fewer options exist on small bodies of water. Here are the steps that I recommend you employ:

1. The key to finding a pattern may be through the quick elimination of much of the pond or canal.

2. Spray-casting deep-running lures is a good way to check out the waters.

3. Once bass are located on structure, then similar areas can be probed.

A thick growth of aquatic weeds often line the shores of these lakes and canals. Thick cover near quick drops usually hold active fish near shore, and a careful approach to such areas is important. Throw parallel to the shoreline initially, and then spray cast the deeper haunts. Bridges can often be found on such waterways. In both man-made and natural waters, deeper waters off sharp drops often hold more bass than do shallow waters.

There are several keys to finding bass and good structure in urban waters. Here are some:

- For a topographical drop, check out the slope of the land, although the fancy landscaping of some developments can deceive even the most knowledgeable bass angler.

- Good depth changes just don't exist in many waterways, so bass rely heavily on the weed habitat present.

- Dense vegetation usually offers ideal pH values and cover for forage and predator fish. The wise angler will fish the densest cover first and then move to isolated clumps or smaller weedbeds.

- Thick weedlines may define a structural break or dropoff, so casts into the vegetation, alongside it, and even 10 feet off toward the deeper water can produce.

URBAN   BASS

The author recommends you try development waters for overlooked bass.

Check out the tips below!

The mouths of any tributaries can be very good early in the year. Concentrate on the emergent vegetation and/or rocky areas in the spring and any submerged wood or brush in the summer. Any points or projections off any islands or canals entering a small body of water can hold bass year around.

The thickest weed areas may hold the most fish, but they can be difficult to fish. Holes in the vegetated thickets are spots the skilled caster can hit, and these pockets generally produce excellent bass fishing. Other ambush points for largemouth bass could include points and changes in type of vegetation.

How To Approach Urban Waterways

Regardless of my common sight on the little development canal mentioned above, most developed areas have less snakes and alligators than more remote waters. That makes them easier for the wade fisherman or bank caster to fish. Manicured shorelines and bulkheads sometimes discourage extensive aquatic weed growth, so wild creatures normally seek other habitat. The presence of people along the shore may also prompt wildlife to relocate elsewhere.

Fishing from the shoreline can be rewarding in terms of family participation, and many novices and beginners can easily fish these waters with a minimum of preparation and equipment. It's a whole-family opportunity, and youngsters can enjoy angling in nearby surroundings without a long trip to larger, more commercialized waters.

Small two-man boats are ideal for most waters. The fishermen can quietly sneak around small lakes and canals with the lightweight craft, simply propelled by small electric motors. It is best to bring your own small boat to such places, because rentals just don't exist. Boat ramps for larger rigs are nonexistent on these waterways, so launch your own miniature fishing rig from the shore, or wade at your leisure.

Easy Access Can Mean More Fishing Opportunities

The small development ponds and lakes are seldom affected by winds. In extremely rough weather, it is usually easier to fish from the shoreline, rather than from a boat bouncing in the waves. Landscaped lakes and canals are much easier to bank fish and less messy in terms of mud, weeds, trees, etc. Their accessibility, in fact, allows a one-hour angling session in street clothes on the way home from work. Stealth is still required since ground vibrations from a bank caster stomping along in hard soled shoes may spook cautious fish in these waterways.

Water visibility can vary greatly and be used to the angler's advantage. Murky or stained waters are normally an excellent cloak for approaching a pond that you have never fished. Few fishermen will want to crawl across a sand trap or putting green to sneak up on their honey hole. Such fun-and-games are possible, though, for an avid bassman working or living close to metropolitan waterways.

Urban dwellers, and there are a bunch, usually need only look a few blocks (or miles) to discover some unforgettable bass action. Most suburb largemouth are overlooked by the angling community, and the hot-weather country club set could care less. That leaves more for us!

RIGGING FOR DEVELOPMENT WATERS

Most anglers in the state have easy access to golf course and real estate development ponds, lakes and canals. When fishing such waters, careful attention should be given to all tackle, including rod and reel, lures, line and accessories.

The development fisherman must be prepared and be equipped right. The four rules of thumb that I use are:

1. travel light; 2. rig light; 3. "string" light; 4. toss light.

These domestic lakes and canals require small boats with very limited tackle storage, or the foot approach (wading or bank walking) which has a severe weight penalty for additional outfits and tackle. Either way, the brute force technique of carrying along seven rods and reels, four tackle boxes and other items (cooler, camera, etc.) just won't work. These waters are made for those who travel light and go prepared.

Never have there been waters created so perfectly for the light tackle angler. Ultralight equipment is well suited for these areas and can be used to corral some awful big bass. When hooked, many of the largest bass will head toward the deepest water available. This gives the angler who rigs light more time to whip the bass in the normally snag-free environment, and the mini-rigs are up to the task.

Line testing 6 to 10 pounds is usually adequate for development and golf club waters. Even the 10 pounders can be handled on the light lines since heavy cover is usually limited. The smaller waters dictate the quiet, careful approach and a line diameter which infringes minimally upon their territory.

- Lunkers from the fairways are partial to the light weights. Bass from small waters are acclimated toward smaller forage, and the smart fisherman will select his lures accordingly.

- Small spinnerbaits, mini crankbaits, injured-minnow plugs and six-inch worms take their toll on these largemouth.

- Consider lures that closely resemble two to three-inch forage such as small minnows, crayfish, insects and frogs.

- Leave the six-inch top water plugs, the 10-inch plastic eels and salt-water sized plugs at home.

Line clippers and a fishing vest may prepare the angler for most eventualities on development water. The successful angler here will always be prepared, but will normally go light!

Larry Larsen on Bass Tactics

CHAPTER 12

HOW TO WIN
WIND BATTLES

Controlling the boat and the cast are keys to effective angling in high winds

White caps are not a pleasant sight to most anglers, yet for those who learn to battle the wind-created environment, bass rewards can be great. The conditions influenced by strong winds differ greatly from those regularly found on most waters. Given the new variables, smart anglers develop a wind strategy that pays off.

I'll usually fish windy banks until I can't hold the boat off them any longer. If the winds are too excessive, then I'll look for a slightly calmer area and throw what I can. Given the choice of a windward shore and a leeward shore, I'll almost always opt for the windy banks. Why? There are several very good reasons why windward banks generally provide the best fishing.

1. The turbulence there stirs up the water and the bait.

2. Strong winds actually produce cover for the bass; the waves and wash make the fish less spooky.

3. An angler can move in tighter to the fish and throw tight-line baits, such as spinnerbaits, crankbaits and "streaking" worm rigs. Such baits are most effective when the bass are positioned by the wind.

Bass will move up onto points if the wind has set up a current across them. They will position according to that current and move up to feed. The tight-line baits then will produce quite well.

How To Position The Boat On A Windward Target

If I'm unable to move the boat into the wind via the electric motor, I'll position it with nose into the wind. I'll leave the trolling motor running on high speed and cast to the side, or toward the back. Sometimes, I am able to fish the spot as I drift backwards with the wind.

If a directionally-oriented weedline exists and the wind strength and direction are right, you can drift along with the wind. The trolling motor should be used just to maintain the position of the boat during the drift. If the lake has scattered weeds, you can still use the electric.

Assuming the weeds are extremely dense, however, a strong wind can actually help move the boat. Normally then, it is difficult to move the boat through vegetation without getting the trolling motor prop entangled. If you do move through the weed beds, the electric may just make a lot of noise and scare the bass. Here's what to do:

1. In a strong wind, run the boat upwind to the head of a massive weed clump, and then shut off the gasoline engine.

2. Fish the vegetation as the wind blows the boat through quietly, without using the trolling motor.

Casting Tips For Keeping The Bait In The Strike Zone

Wind-blown anglers often are faced with casting problems unless every toss happens to be with the wind. Level wind baitcasting reels are suited for the tight-line baits, but they tend to backlash when casting light lures into the teeth of a strong wind. While they are more difficult to use in high winds, they allow more versatility when using bigger baits.

Spinning and spin-cast gear are a little more forgiving and popular under such conditions. They are easier to cast, but neither is wind-proof. In windy conditions, about the only way to toss finesse baits, like a small Rapala or Gitzit, is with the open- or close-face spin tackle. There are several things to keep in mind, though, when using spinning gear.

● The line is coming off the reel in much larger coils than in traditional baitcasting. Consequently, the wind has a longer time to act on the coils, and they can blow around. That diminishes the ease of their funneling into the first guide, and that can be a problem.

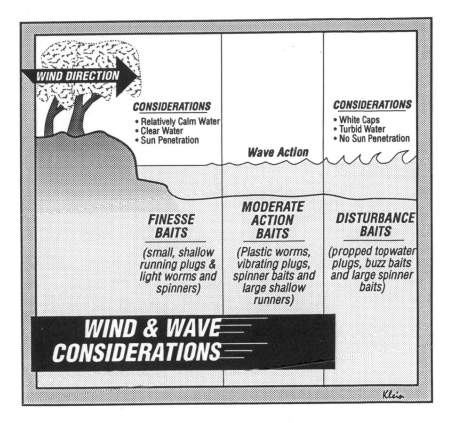

CONSIDERATIONS
- Relatively Calm Water
- Clear Water
- Sun Penetration

CONSIDERATIONS
- White Caps
- Turbid Water
- No Sun Penetration

WIND DIRECTION

Wave Action

FINESSE BAITS

(small, shallow running plugs & light worms and spinners)

MODERATE ACTION BAITS

(Plastic worms, vibrating plugs, spinner baits and large shallow runners)

DISTURBANCE BAITS

(propped topwater plugs, buzz baits and large spinner baits)

WIND & WAVE CONSIDERATIONS

- The best way to combat large coils of line blowing in the wind is to go to smaller diameter or lighter test lines, and/or to heavier, tight-line lures. The latter results in the line being pulled out more quickly and helps to keep the line taut during the retrieve.

- A line with a large surface area will be susceptible to a tremendous bow in the wind and in the water. Whatever you see happening above water is also happening to an equal extent underwater. We can crank in the slack and remove what the wind has done, but we will still have a tremendous bow in the line under the water that's not seen.

The whole problem with the bow in your line due to wind above water and water resistance beneath the surface is that you are not straight to your lure. You lose feel and sensitivity, and you won't be able to achieve good hook sets. To get around that, you would want to go to ultra limp lines that are smaller in diameter, such as

How To Win Wind Battles

85

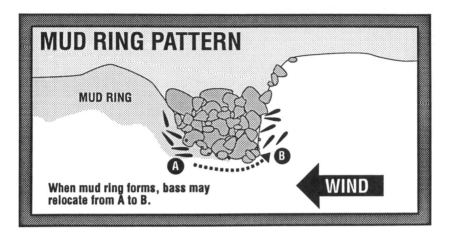

MUD RING PATTERN

MUD RING

When mud ring forms, bass may relocate from A to B.

WIND

Trilene XL or UltraThin as opposed to Trilene XT which is less flexible.

How To Select And Present The Lure In A Gale

If you go to a smaller line diameter in a wind, you may be able to throw the small to mid-size lures. If you stay with the same size and diameter line in a gale, then you probably should use a heavier lure. The heavier lure will cast out more quickly and give the line less time in the air.

Here are some additional important tips:

- If you are making long distance casts, you want to shorten your casts in windy situations. Get closer to the fish, and you no longer have to contend with extra line blowing around.

- You need to be sneakier or quieter when conducting warfare from such close range.

- You may want to go to a longer rod to help project the line out into the wind better.

- You may also want to go to a lighter action rod with a quicker tip; that will let you shoot your line and lure out more quickly through the air.

When Conditions Dictate Lure Presentation

When the bass are concentrated on a breakline, point or underwater hump, I'll often toss a heavy crankbait into the wind. The weight of the lure and applying appropriate thumb pressure on the

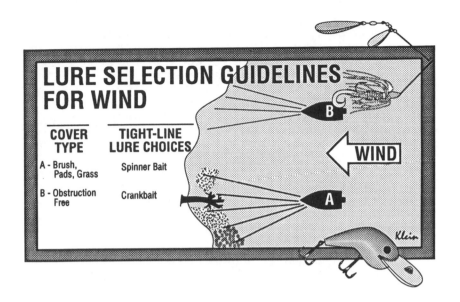

LURE SELECTION GUIDELINES FOR WIND

COVER TYPE	TIGHT-LINE LURE CHOICES
A - Brush, Pads, Grass	Spinner Bait
B - Obstruction Free	Crankbait

WIND

B

A

Klein

casting spool at the right time allows me to do that. The lure coming back with the wind will resemble a baitfish being "washed back" over the point or hump.

If the water conditions are extremely clear, you can position the boat up wind of the area and cast with the wind. You can get more distance on your cast that way.

In heavy winds, I'll work the points thoroughly. I'll work any boat cuts through a grass bed, because a current will often be set up through them. If a strong wind is blowing from the north, for example, the south end of the lake will get a pile of water built up. That will set up strong currents in cuts on that side, and fishing the mouths of those cuts will be extremely productive. Under such conditions, I will just move from cut to cut. The winds and water movement make the bass active.

How To Operate The Trolling Motor

If the wind is extremely strong and the wave action is forcing the bow of the boat up to where the trolling motor prop leaves the water, it must be operated intermittently. A prop that leaves the water with each wave and cavitates, makes a lot of noise. The easiest way to handle that is to simply take your foot off the switch as the prop leaves the water, and then step on it once the prop is again in the water.

In high winds, operating a trolling motor can sometimes be a task. For ease of operation, most anglers need some sort of seat in the bow of the boat, whether it be a pedestal seat or a bicycle-type seat, sometimes called a "pro pole". For anglers who fish standing up, the latter will allow him to lean on it for stabilization. He'll be able to fish more effectively while operating the trolling motor.

An angler that can brace himself against the bow seat is usually able to handle most waves that he would face on a windy day. Those anglers that leave the bow seat behind and try to balance themselves in heavy wave action are usually sorry.

Winds don't have to scare an angler. Use common sense for safety purposes and intelligence for boat positioning and lure presentation, and the catch is almost assured.

CHAPTER 13
WHIPPING WIND, WAVES & WAKES
How to catch feeding bass in the teeth of a gale

Pounding winds and a few white caps that inevitably engulf the bow of your bass boat will pose problems. They are known to wreak havoc with established patterns and are responsible for bass movement, rough boating conditions and angler frustration. Regardless of whether we prefer to fish protected waters or not, the fact remains that most anglers will have to fish in windy conditions sooner or later.

I spent 21 years of my life in Kansas, the "wind capital of the United States." There, wind was a part of life. When I moved, I expected to find calm waters. I've lived in four states and fished another 20 states and about that many other countries, and have yet to see optimal wind conditions for more than a day or two in succession.

Flatland lakes are normally shallow, unprotected and thus easily affected by the wind. The low land and roundness of the typical natural lakes allow the wind factor to be more prominent than in other hilly areas. Reservoirs in the hills or mountains are often large, and even they are affected by winds.

On round-shaped lakes, winds from any direction can be beneficial by 'stirring' up the lake into a more homogeneous body. Pockets of dead water, for example, are seldom found in a shallow lake. Such wind-caused turbulence can be beneficial to the fishery and the lake.

Even though spring fish may be back in the coves on large reservoirs, a wind can tend to "pull" bass out to the points. The dingy water along the shorelines also encourages largemouth to move to the windy banks in that cove. Food in the stirred up environment is the attraction.

How The Food Chain Attracts Bass

Success on wind-blown waters of all types can usually be attributed to the wave action stirring up sediments and food sources for small organisms. Bass are drawn to such areas to feed with confidence because of the "cover" of waves and resulting muddied water.

Water movement, created by wind, waves and wakes, may collect baitfish and is a key to effectively catching wind-blown bass. Small pockets or coves just off the main lake are great spots when the wind is blowing into them. Why?

1. The wind blows plankton into these areas.

2. Shad feed on the plankton.

3. Bass in that area become active and feed on the shad.

When the wind direction is perpendicular to a bridge, the current is forced through the pilings. Forage is then washed through the bridge area, which attracts the bass. Wind will blow schools of shad around and wash crayfish out of shoreline rocks. For similar food chain reasons, sea wall breaks and culverts are productive.

A cut into a creek from a shallow bay is another forage-attractive spot during high winds. It should be fished by casting the lure into the cut and bringing it out with the current. Further information on specific bait use can be found in the book, "Bass Guide Tips", which is book 9 in the BASS SERIES LIBRARY. Ordering details can be found at the back of this book.

How To Use The Anchor In The Approach

A key piece of equipment for productive angling in the wind is the anchor. It must be used effectively, however, to aid your fishing. You won't need to have a foot on the trolling motor at all times if you use the anchors in your storage compartment.

Wind can influence the fishing, and anchors can be valuable, as a friend and I found out years ago on a small Central Florida lake. The warm May weekend had followed several days of very mild winds. We expected the trend to continue, but the wind came up suddenly while we were on the lake. The water surface became turbulent. The waves pounded the pad beds, but were dampened as they penetrated further into the bed.

Success on wind-blown waters of all types can usually be attributed to the wave action stirring up sediments and food sources for small organisms. Bass are drawn to such areas to feed. Fishing drop baits, such as worms, requires a very sensitive "feel". In high winds, it can be difficult detecting strikes.

We moved immediately to the windward shore where we located another bed of lily pads in about three feet of water. It was being lashed by the white caps, so we approached slowly. The exterior pads were quite heavy and afforded the inner pad area some calmness. Anchors at both ends of the boat allowed us to thoroughly cast the outside edge of the pads.

Here's the anchoring/fishing strategy that worked:

1. Our plastic worms crawled along on the top of the leaves, falling into the open water pockets every once in a while. After six or seven retrieves each, we lifted our anchors and let the waves push us another 10 feet toward the pad bed.

2. We dropped the anchors and cast our lures to the pad holes deeper in the bed. Another 10 feet closer seemed to make the difference.

A six-pound bass gobbled up my chunky black plastic as it hit the water. She exploded on the surface about 20 feet back into the pads. I gingerly pressured her through both the pad entanglements and the whitecaps to the net. On my next cast, the lure disappeared into a swirl that formed beneath on the outskirts of the bed. I hauled a four-pound bass aboard.

Three casts later, as my lure "crawled" up on a pad leaf, there was a large boil just behind it. I twitched the rod tip "walking" the lure about 10 feet before it finally fell from the leaves into the water. The chunky 5 1/4-pounder seemed to anticipate its touching down, as the strike was instantaneous. All three fish were my

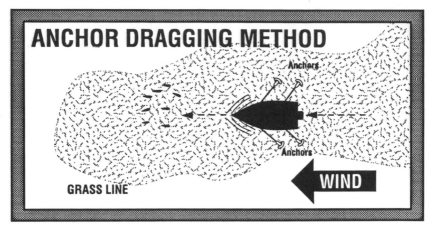

Anchor-dragging is not a "run and gun" method; it is not an effective way to locate bass quickly. When using this relatively slow technique, you should have an idea of where the bass are concentrated beforehand. It is difficult to locate large numbers of active bass in heavy cover with a strong wind blowing.

photo subjects before being released. Not all windy days are as productive.

When To Drag Anchors To Catch More Bass

Wind speed on large waters can increase quickly, and one way to battle a rough "sea" when fishing is to actually drag two anchors through the cover. Even then, the boat may be moving too fast through the area. Drop a couple more anchors until the boat's speed is adjusted to accommodate your casts.

While it is very difficult to hold the boat in high winds in order to catch bass, this technique stands out. Here's the plan:

- Cast a plastic worm with the wind ahead of your boat's drift.

- While drifting toward the bait, work it as you would in flipping, with a jigging motion.

- Reel in the slack as you go and take up any remaining before you set the hook.

This method is not a "run and gun" method; it is not an effective way to quickly locate bass. When using this relatively slow technique, you should have an idea of where the bass are

LURES FOR WINDY SITUATIONS

Productive wind battlers usually prefer lures that most closely imitate the baitfish that are being blown up on the banks. In high winds, they also opt for the tight-line lures, ones that can just be cast and retrieved, such as spinnerbaits, vibrating plugs and crankbaits.

Spinnerbaits are ideal for working the weeds, reeds, moss, brush, trees, etc., to minimize hangups. Chartreuse, white, yellow, black or combinations of those hues work well. Under windy conditions, run a trailer hook on the spinnerbait so that the bass has a better chance at making contact.

Vibrating baits are excellent "active" lures for oft times active fish. If the bank is fairly obstruction-free, use a crankbait under the whitecaps. The lure is normally fairly weedless in heavy cover if you keep it moving at all times with a medium-fast retrieve.

Large lures are especially effective in heavy wind and wave action. In a howling storm, the additional noise will attract trophy-size fish. Big baits should be cast against the wind when possible. They are retrieved in the same direction as the waves.

Sometimes, anglers have difficulty when fishing drop baits, such as worms or jigs, in the wind. Using such lures during a wind-whipping session requires a very sensitive "feel", and you have to be aware of the difficulty in detecting strikes then. When anchored on a spot, though, the slower baits can be extremely productive.

concentrated beforehand. It is difficult to locate large numbers of active bass in heavy cover with a strong wind blowing.

How To Use The Guise of Filtered Sun

The windy shore usually offers decreased visibility due to less light penetrating the surface layer of the lake. Under the guise of surface-disturbing waves, flats with underwater vegetation, sediment or stumps and an incoming wind can be productive spots. Here's why:

- When the wind is blowing into a shoreline, especially on a clear lake, that shore is being stirred up and a mud ring may develop.

- Once the muddy water appears, bass in nearby cover believe that forage may be washed out of rocks. Those bass will then feed.

Whipping Wind, Waves & Wakes   93

I'll generally opt for areas, such as points, submerged islands and creek channels, where the wind direction is perpendicular to the potential structure. When the wind blows directly into a point, for example, the fishing is not usually as good as it is when the wind is blowing across it.

Bass will usually lie on the deeper or opposite side of a point waiting for baitfish. There will usually be a current flowing across these places, and bass will often be in dingier water just behind the point facing the current to catch bait coming over or around them. Periodic winds, waves and wakes make this a reality.

CHAPTER 14

CRANK UP THE OUTBOARD
How to troll to locate and catch bigger fish

My mother's rod had buckled with the obvious strain of a heavy fish. I threw the outboard into neutral, jumped up from my "guide" position behind the steering wheel, and grabbed the over-sized net.

She struggled to lead a leaping largemouth to the gunnel. That bass, though, wasn't going to let her close the distance between them too fast. The fish bulled toward the nearby hydrilla, but was snubbed short.

The largemouth jumped again, trying to throw the crankbait that got it into that mess. My mom hung on.

Three or four minutes of battle ensued and passed as the 100 yards of line was reduced to a few feet. My father, who had reeled in his lure to prevent any entanglements, grabbed the steering wheel and throttle control to keep the bow pointed into the 15 mph wind. I leaned out to capture the heavyweight and swung it aboard.

The seven-and-one-half-pound largemouth was a healthy specimen, obviously full of roe. It was my mother's largest bass ever and, to date, her most memorable angling experience.

Productive Passes With Crankbaits

We had started fishing at 3 p.m. and had been trolling for only five minutes. The trophy jumped on the Rebel crankbait as we made our first pass over a submerged hump in a spring-fed central Florida lake.

On the next pass, my father set the hook into a small, two-pound largemouth. I turned the boat for a third pass and my parents again free-spooled their lures back some 50 to 80 yards behind the boat. As we passed the hump, which was about eight feet deep on top, the drag on my mother's reel again sounded as the rod flexed and vibrated with something alive at the other end of the line.

A four-pounder took to the sky trying to shake the terminal hardware, but to no avail. The bass was brought to the boat, and soon, it was resting comfortably in the treated, live well water. A dose of Catch-And-Release formula mixed with the lake water helps the fish maintain their protective slime coat and retards any fungus that may be initiated in the handling process.

How To Locate Bass In A Wet Weed Field

Three passes and three nice bass is not bad action for an afternoon trolling trip. My parents again placed their crankbaits off the stern and I steered my 18-foot boat towards our productive hump. Peering at the chart recorder, it was relatively easy to find. Here's what was there:

- The bottom surrounding the hump was 15 feet on one side and 20 to 24 feet on the other three.

- A couple of feet of hydrilla hugged the shallowest part of the hump.

- Some 20 feet away from the hump, a bank of the dense vegetation lay in protection of the distant shoreline. That piece of structure had everything, including the fish.

- Inverted V's on the graph paper revealed the presence of fish.

We started pass number four, and I confidently cautioned my parents to hang onto their rods. There were more bass there.

Boat Operation Can Be The Key To Catching Bass

As their lures approached the hump, I moved the throttle to neutral momentarily to slow the speed. My confidence as a guide boosted, I boldly predicted another fish. I had just gotten the words "right now" out of my mouth when the crankbait on my father's side changed directions. The lure's forward momentum abruptly halted and the line cut a path toward shoreline.

"It's just a small one," my father repeated over and over, as he struggled to refill his casting spool. The largemouth wasn't that little. The hefty five-and-one-half-pounder wanted to keep its distance from the boat.

The 50 yards of 17-pound test monofilament was soon gathered up, and I swung the net under a nice bass. We made a final pass on the hump without success, and with the skies clouding up, my thoughts turned to gathering a few photos before the late afternoon sun disappeared.

I snapped photos of the victorious anglers, and we slipped all the bass back into the lake. They quickly swam off to recuperate, feed, and grow, and be ready for battle on another day.

For my parents, then in their youthful 70's, this brief trolling experience was a means to find quick action. They won't soon forget it. For the Wichita, Kansas residents, it was easily the highlight of their visit with me that year.

How To Troll More Effectively

Effective trolling is not simply a matter of letting out lures and motoring around a lake. To be successful, the angler has to be concerned with several things. Here's just a short list:

- motor speed

- lure depth (and size)

- water depth

- changes in topography

- vegetation present

- wind direction and velocity

- structure available

- potential hangups present

- trolling tackle (including rod, reel, and line)

Trolling shallow, highly vegetated waters is often very difficult. Too many things can disrupt the intention. Frequent snags or weed catches can frustrate the beginning troller, but for those with an inordinate amount of patience and a little smarts, a virtually untapped 'gold mine' exists.

There are ways to maneuver around potential hangups, but the successful bass troller has to be near them. That's generally where the bigger fish are. Largemouth are structure-oriented, even away from the shoreline.

Know Your Speed Variations And Repeatability

Spced is a variable, and the motor should be able to handle from extremely slow to fairly fast (four or five miles per hour) speeds. For trolling live shiners or plastic worms, an electric motor is better suited. But for pulling crankbaits and maximizing the coverage fast, the gasoline version is ideal.

The outboard used for trolling can literally be any size. Even my 150 XP idles down enough to find the bass. It works for me.

The real key to producing several strikes with an outboard is being able to cover the same area at the exact speed that generated the previous strikes. Consistency here is vital.

Don't Forget The Right Equipment For Trolling

To be productive, the troller must have the proper equipment. Most boats will work fine. Here are some of the key components to a good trolling set up:

1. Padded swivel seats are a comfort that I can't do without, but the only essential boat criteria is that the anglers can face the action, with head turned. This is to ensure that the fisherman is constantly aware of what his lure is doing, and to facilitate a proper hook set.

2. A tachometer is an important aid in keeping the baits running through the hot spot at the same depth and speed. If the plug drew a strike when being trolled at 1000 rpm's, then another chance at a largemouth should come by throttling the outboard once again to that mark, and retracing the productive steps.

3. An essential piece of equipment for the productive troller is a good depth finder, preferably a chart recorder type, rather than a flasher or LCD unit. The graph gives a permanent readout for those with a short memory.

My boat is equipped with a dash-mounted Lowrance X16 for painting a picture of the bottom while using the outboard. For spotting bottom characteristics when relying on my bow-mounted electric, I've got a Bottom Line Sidefinder. Both are valuable tools for locating largemouth, and the most productive paths for their contact.

CHAPTER 15

TROLLING THE CONCENTRATIONS
How to develop a productive system for more bass

Trolling crankbaits over and around vegetation is just one effective way to catch bass from big concentrations. I utilized such a technique several times over the years in Texas on Fayette County Lake, and it regularly caught largemouth and lots of them.

Hydrilla-covered points and humps provide productive haunts for bass concentrations, but fishing them can be frustrating. Hangups, at least temporary ones, are a way of life. In trolling such areas, they can be counted on to interrupt the operation, but you can learn to overlook such.

I made six passes of the first point to the right of the ramp at Fayette one day and had several interruptions to my troll. Eighteen were largemouth bass which were quickly landed and released. Five would have easily bested the 16-inch minimum in force at the time.

With each trolling pass that day, I became more familiar with the "lay of the land" beneath the boat. Hangups became less frequent and the bass picking better. My eyes were trained on the chart recorder with each pass, and I was learning to fish the hydrilla points and humps off that shoreline.

My shad-colored crankbaits ran at about 8 feet and that's where the bass were located that day. Since then, I've used trolling as an effective method to fish vegetation in lakes around the country. It may not be as exciting as other methods, but it can be more productive at times, depending on the type of cover and the location of the largemouth.

How To Use Location Tactics For Big Bass

Location of bass concentrations is what trolling is about. Usually too, the average size largemouth caught with the outboard in use is much larger than what comes from shoreline casting. Trolling is a big fish technique, and one that I often use when after a better class of largemouth.

Of the hundreds of largemouth that I've caught with trolled lures, the resultant average weight is probably a respectable 3 1/2 pounds, about twice what my lure tossing has accomplished. Why? There are several reasons or "truths" to understand.

1. Big bass will often hang tight to cover, making their strike zone difficult to reach unless the lure tracks nearby.

2. Wind and vegetation may dictate the productive approach. Often, largemouth will hit the lure when presented from only one direction. The smart troller will quickly note that, and circle back to repeat the path. A concentration can be effectively worked in this manner.

3. Offshore cover and topographical changes are not always easy to find, particularly in natural lakes. But they do exist.

It may take a few gallons of gas to pinpoint a spot with the most potential, but time just looking is usually well spent. Submerged weed-covered bars and humps are my favorite way to a few fat largemouth. Creek channels, rock outcroppings, and almost any breakline are productive. Most lakes have them, and rivers of all sizes are full of that type structure.

How To Mark Spots And Repeat Your Troll-By

Unless you know the waters or can quickly chart the spots on which you are going to focus, marker buoys are helpful. When a few fish on structure are spotted on the depth finder, toss over a weighted marker. On any strike do the same. Remember which buoy marks fish and which one marks the boat location when one was contacted.

With a chart recorder, it is easy to relate time and distance as you pass over a fish and entice a strike 80 feet later.

The successful troller should be able to return his lure to its productive position, once established. To catch more than one fish from a concentration, you will want to consider the following:

• Repeat the course of travel after marking a strike, and be ready as you approach the buoy. A second bass may hit the lure early or late.

Trolling is an extremely effective method for locating bass quickly, even on shallow waters with submerged vegetation.

- Have your line out the same distance during each pass to eliminate that variable. The best way to accomplish this is by marking your line at that point with a waterproof marker.

- Another way to repeat a productive line distance is to use a different color marker for each 25 feet and remember what each stands for. As an example, use a red marker every 50 feet, and a green one to mark the line mid-way between the red marks.

Remember To Keep The Lure Tight To Cover

I've found that lures moving within a couple of feet of the bottom structure will result in more strikes than those combing shallower areas. Big bass, in particular, lie near heavy cover.

On a recent trip, I trolled right into a hydrilla mass which grew to within three feet of the surface. Deep obstruction-free waters hugged both sides of the weedbed. My first two passes over the structure resulted in a hangup and a clog of vegetation being 'horsed' to boatside. The third pass resulted in a seven-pounder that grabbed my shad-replica crankbait just before it reached the hyacinth bed.

That spot, like most of the better ones found by trolling, are off the shoreline for several reasons:

1. The banks are beaten to death in many cases, and often the primary concentrations of big bass are found in waters away from the nearest shore.

2. Offshore fish rarely see a lure pass by their main habitat.

3. Largemouth living in the depths away from the banks are not affected by shoreline pressure, unless on a feeding jaunt into the shallows or while spawning.

Sizing The Baits And Line For More Bass

The offshore trophies are usually gluttons for big baits or lures. The trolled plug is a critical part of the package offered the bass. A billed crankbait that dives to 8 feet when retrieved after a 50-foot cast can usually be trolled at 12-foot depths at the end of a couple hundred feet of light line. A line testing 30 pounds is more buoyant, and has additional drag. It would possibly limit the lure's descent on a short cast to five feet or so.

The productive trolling system relies on the right combination of lure, line size and length, and boat speed. Used over the right haunts, it's often successful. Here's the basis for attracting more bass to your trolled offering:

- Longer lengths of line allow the lure to run slightly deeper.

- Lure size, buoyancy, lip angle and lip size are parameters that affect the system. Bigger baits may be more buoyant but a deep-diving lip will put them down to the strike zone.

- Deeper fish seem to go after larger lures too.

Bigger bass are offshore. Most "outboard anglers" know that. While not offering the same kind of excitement available to those trolling the shoreline, the thrills are many.

Larry Larsen on Bass Tactics

CHAPTER 16

WILY WADER WAYS
How to effectively probe shallow ponds and lakes

The pond's muddy bottom sucked at my chest-high waders as my fishing partner and I carefully made our way toward our selected spots to make our first cast. The tandem blades clattered as I lofted a cast into the brisk wind. The spinnerbait touched down 20 feet in front of me near some emerging pickerel weed.

I had just started my retrieve, slowly crawling the lure along the silted pond bed, when a fat, four-pound largemouth struck the bait. She boiled on the pond's choppy surface and charged for the nearby weeds. The waves lapped at the top of my waders as I stumbled backward, heading for shallower waters.

The battle continued, and once I reached knee-deep water, the fight was more on my terms. I leveraged the bass from two weed bed entanglements and finally worked her close enough to grab her jaw.

I waded out again and continued to cast the four-acre sandhill pond. The chartreuse bait attracted a second strike from the same productive spot. The quick repeat performance interested my fishing partner, who moved nearby to help me fish the productive underwater spot. We stood side by side on the point in belly-button-deep water and quickly hooked two more fat bass. With their bellies full of threadfin shad, the feisty bass fought "heavier" than their two- to three-pound weights.

Wading well out into the shallow pond could be accomplished only on one of two points projecting into the water. Not surprising, the bass were on that submerged point in sparse weed beds covered mostly by five feet of water. That pond was fairly typical, in terms of habitat and wadeability.

Focus On Small Bodies of Water

In a small, shallow pond or cove, a wade fisherman can outfish any angler on the bank or in a boat. Fortunately, there are many relatively shallow lakes, ponds and rivers throughout the country that present wading opportunities. Some reservoirs and rivers in hill country are extremely deep, but many smaller tributaries, ponds and even coves of the large reservoirs contain accessible water for the wade fisherman.

Just how productive wading the small waters can be was proven to me when I was just 17 years old. My brother and two older friends had accompanied me to a one-acre farm pond belonging to a relative. The four of us waded the brush-filled waters wearing old tennis shoes and blue jeans. We were waist deep most of the time, as we cast side by side to both visible structures and the open water in front of the dam. Our baits were the same, and even our line was of similar test. The results were not.

Our combined catch totaled maybe 50 bass, most of which were small, but I was doing something right. The six largemouth keepers which ranged from two to five pounds all hit my injured-minnow lure. The stringer clipped to my belt loop was impressive. My compadres tossing into the same spots ahead of me were confounded with the results, or their lack of results. One of them, an outdoor writer for the Wichita Eagle/Beacon, referred to the events as "all luck" in his column the following day.

I certainly can't say that landing the only large fish was all skill, but something was subtly different. Our retrieve rates appeared the same, but my spinning reel might have had a different retrieve ratio, causing a lure speed difference. My sense of feel might have detected the strikes better. Who knows? Regardless, my partners' imitations of the productive technique that afternoon were to no avail.

Although the size of the water has little to do with its wadeability, smaller tributaries, ponds and shallow coves lend themselves more easily to the wade fishing technique. One can be more in touch with those waters.

Where You Should Look For Natural Signs

Although I was able to figure out where that pond's shallow water was located, sometimes a careful search is required. The surface expression of the habitat does not always indicate what lies beneath the water's surface. The bank terrain and emergent vegetation may be similar, but bottom topography may not be conducive to wading.

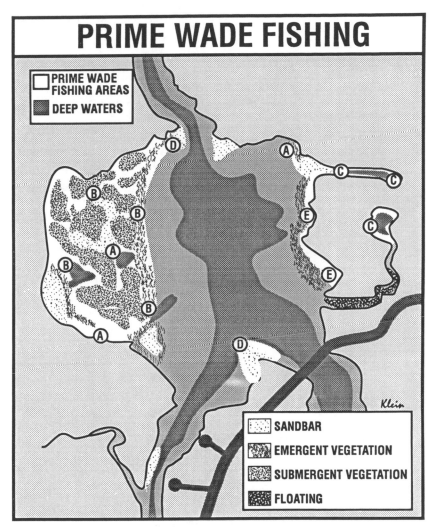

PRIME WADE FISHING

PRIME WADE FISHING AREAS

DEEP WATERS

SANDBAR

EMERGENT VEGETATION

SUBMERGENT VEGETATION

FLOATING

Some of the key areas that waders should consider are shown in this sketch of a typical lake. A - Any vegetation, emergent or submergent, with nearby deep water access should denote productive areas. B - Boat trails and cuts through vegetation would be great habitat for largemouth. C - Wadeable areas with adjacent deep water that are protected by sandbars or floating vegetation (which block boat traffic) should be tried. D - Points into the lake always deserve attention. E - A perimeter slough behind an impenetrable wall of emergent vegetation is an ideal protected, wade fishing area.

Rather than jump into a body of water as a method to find out its depth, there are certain "natural" signs that may help determine its wadeability.

- Flooded trees a few yards from shore could indicate shallow waters.

- By studying the size of their trunks you can often estimate the depth of the water at their base and determine whether or not it is shallow enough to wade.

- If the banks of the cove are composed of rocks and submerged tree tops, you can pretty well be sure that it contains a deep shoreline.

To find an arm of a lake with wadeable water, I'll carefully note the emergent structure such as trees, weeds and other plant life, and then attempt to figure out the depth of water beneath it. Coves with plenty of vegetation and small flooded timber are usually a good bet to fish.

You Should See The Forests and The Trees

If the lake's cove has a marshy shoreline and shallower shores than others around the lake, wade fishing can be very productive. Emergent trees in a reservoir cove can clue you in on the depths present...before you get you feet wet.

Trees usually grow on the highest ground, so those along the bank of a cove should denote a gradual slope to deeper water. If the trees are in the middle of a cove, that may be where the shallower water lies.

- An extremely deep cove with waters too deep to wade may be revealed by the tops of submerged trees projecting above the lake's surface very near the shoreline.

- A lack of trees near the shore and in the water sometimes denotes shallower, low-lying lands with very little drop.

- The fertility of the soil and water drainage characteristics usually dictate what trees will grow in the area.

- Although a boat is not required for most wading activity, it can be used to reach a shallow cove or wadeable spot on the far shore of a small lake. Not surprisingly, many bass chasers with big, expensive rigs take to the water for some "wet" angling. Several boating friends even prefer wade fishing over casting from their comfortable floating craft.

Larry Larsen on Bass Tactics

How To Turn Slowness Afoot Into An Advantage

The slowness afoot involved in wade fishing can be an advantage. Wading doesn't allow an angler to cover a lot of ground fast, but it forces him to fish more thoroughly than would the average boat angler. When the lure is presented repeatedly or closer to a bass, usually the better the chances are for a strike.

Systematically approaching a wadeable area is one of the best ways to locate largemouth. Here's a couple of approaches:

1. Unless it is a very new impoundment, you may be able to obtain bottom contour maps to help in choosing the areas to wade.

2. If maps aren't handy, a boat and good depth finder or long pole is useful. A small lake can usually be charted for wade fishing in a short time, but a larger one may require some time.

Wading is an effective way to check out any body of water. A friend and I were once fishing a small lake with abundant flooded timber. The small trees projecting above the surface actually interfered with our boat maneuvering and as a result, wade fishing proved to be the most effective method for those waters. We checked the depth with a flasher first by boat. We sketched a rough contour map and, once familiar with the relative depths, began to methodically work the timber closest to deep, unwadeable water.

After five hours of stumbling through the flooded brush, we had caught two 6-pound largemouth and 12 others between two and six pounds. Four follow-up trips resulted in similar catches and enjoyment. For that lake, wade fishing was the only way to go.

How Temperature Variances Can Mean More Bass

Wading a lake is also an excellent way to keep tabs on water temperature variances. We found numerous areas of thermal difference moving about the muddy waters of that small lake. Most denoted an elevation change of only a couple of feet. Although we wore blue jeans and tennis shoes, a temperature difference can often be detected even through nylon-covered rubber waders.

Bass react to variations in temperature, structure, and pH and oxygen values. The wader can often find the structure and thermal variance without electronic equipment. A change in structure could be a change from pickerel grass to bulrushes or to eel grass, and bass concentrations inhabit each of those spots.

Even in cooler weather, wading lakes and ponds should not be overlooked. Temperature differences still exist, and braving the elements can certainly pay off. Many giant bass are taken from cooler waters. Wade fishing then can be a very effective method of catching large numbers of bass.

CHAPTER 17

WADING MOVING WATERS

**How to determine best approaches, baits
and presentations**

Not all wading opportunities occur in lakes and ponds. Rivers
and creeks offer their share of the activity and many are full of
neglected bass. I have waded many creeks that had productive
pools along much of their length. Often such waters have numerous points that discourage boat traffic and fishing pressure.

Many years ago before catch and release was a necessity, I kept
the majority of largemouth that I caught. My stringer was sometimes almost too heavy to carry home. A quarter of a mile walk in
chest-high waders with 30 pounds of bass on his shoulder and an
assortment of tackle is not an easy task for a teenager.

Wade fishing moving waters has not become accepted by bass
anglers as it has been by trout anglers. Therefore, most bass
anglers have not learned how enjoyable wading the serene and
tranquil rivers and creeks can be.

During the summer, when air temperatures of 90 to 95 degrees
can drive bass to great depths in lakes, moving waters can be the
perfect alternative.

• Shore habitat in creeks and rivers generally retains its share of fish,
regardless of depth.

• River bass don't seem to be bothered with the extremes of weather,
as do those in still waters.

• Moving waters that are relatively warm are the better ones to wade,
not only because they are more productive, but also safer. Acciden-
tal falls can be serious when the waters are cold and the currents
swift. Insulated waders and a fishing partner are obviously important when fishing in cool waters.

The Keys To Approaching Bass In The Rivers

Bass in rivers and creeks are usually very accessible to the wade fisherman. They can normally be found holding on structure in shallow water near deep-water protection, within easy reach of the wader. The successful angler has to approach them carefully, though, because shallow water bass spook easily. That's particularly true in the clear waters found in many rivers.

Here are some keys to catching more bass:

- Even in rivers that are predominately deep, a wader can generally cast from the shallow shores to most deep water haunts of the largemouth. An advantage over the bank-bound fisherman is that the wader is seldom prevented from accessing prime spots due to trees on the shore.

- River bass usually lie in the quieter stretches. Largemouth in particular, avoid strong currents, intent on ambushing their prey as it washes by an eddy.

- For the wader, the slower-moving waters are easier and safer to walk through.

- When walking a creek or river bottom, the wader should move slowly and not shuffle his feet. Silt and sand is usually picked up by moving water and can tip off the angler's presence to downstream inhabitants.

Select The Right Baits For Wading

Soft-landing baits are usually most productive in clear river waters. The relatively-closed environment makes any "intrusion" easy to detect by those living within. Even in stained or discolored water, careful wading is recommended in order to keep sound and habitat disturbance to a minimum.

Small spinnerbaits, plastic worms and grubs and crankbaits produce well in small, moving water environments. Many waders prefer single-hook lures for safety reasons when battling a feisty bass up close.

More than once, I've had a powerful largemouth swim between my legs with a bait carrying a pair of treble hooks. That's not a comfortable feeling, I assure you.

Know The Lure Presentation Parameters

In moving waters, lure presentation is vital to assembling a fine catch. Being able to methodically work the baits through a structure from more than one angle is the advantage of a wade fisherman, but he must first understand and adapt to the current.

Several casts to a particular object may be necessary to attract a resident bass, and if the wader allows for the current to sweep his lure correctly, his chances are better.

Accurate casting on rivers and creeks is essential when wade fishing. Fortunately, a wader can control his casts better and work closer to cover than can a boat fisherman.

• Short and accurate casts minimize hangups and produce more bass.

• It's easier to control the lure and set the hook with a short, taut line.

Using The Shadow Factor To Catch More Fish

Although the boat-bound angler generally casts a longer shadow than does the wader, the sun's position is always paramount to success. Knowing how to use shadows to his advantage will help an angler's wading technique.

A wading angler's projected shadow under a bright sun at a low angle may possibly spook nearby bass. Shadows, however, also exist from structure that the fish may be holding on. This provides the best habitat in the river for the quarry, particularly in clear waters. A wader should be aware of the shadowy side of underwater structure as possible bass haunts.

How To Check Out Non-Limiting Bottom Contours

Bass in moving waters feed often. The waters are slightly warmer during cold weather and cooler during hot weather. The metabolism of river bass seems to be high most times, so it is not too difficult to trigger sprees of feeding in the wadeable areas.

• Work deeper areas from the shallow points. Wading in three feet of water and fishing areas that are much deeper may be required. But that is usually very possible from such a position.

• Don't overlook nearby depths. The bottom contours of a river or creek vary, but eight to 10 feet of depth can often be found near a shallow bank.

Obviously, great care should be used when fishing water with possible dropoffs and deeper sections. Effectively casting to some moving waters may be unfeasible, due to the limitations of the casting positions.

Regardless of your choice of waters, wade fishing can be a fun, exciting and productive experience. The time between steps provides the angler with more time in which to contemplate his strategy. And, with bass, you need all the smarts you can muster!

MAP CONSULTATION

Mapping out your angling strategy is paramount to successful wading. In fact, the well-equipped, serious wader will usually consult a map before he heads out. Selecting the waters to wade can often best be determined with a geological survey map.

On many maps, you can determine:

1. Access points

2. Topographic features

3. Special facilities

4. Lake regulations

Some of the best lake and river maps in the country are produced by Fishing Hot Spots of Rhinelander, Wisconsin. They offer waterproof/tearproof contour maps of several thousand waters in a couple dozen states. The maps include boat landings, fishing tips, and even marked fishing spots. They also offer extensive research findings on each body of water that includes vegetation communities, soil type, runoff sources, etc. No other maps offer such complete information to the fisherman. I know, because I was involved in the research and development of the Florida map series for the company. For more information, Fishing Hot Spots can be contacted by calling toll-free 1-800-338-5957.

Maps for most large lakes are available through the controlling authorities (U.S. Army Corps of Engineers/specific river authorities). Topographic maps are available for most areas west of the Mississippi River from the federal government. Write the Department of the Interior, Geological Survey, Distribution Section, Federal Center, Denver, CO 80225.

My three-book "Guide To Florida Bass Waters Series" includes numerous maps and information on average and maximum depths, vegetation habitat and specific areas to find bass in each season. Over 1,000 Florida lakes, rivers and streams are covered in the reference books. North, Central and South Florida guides are available from Larsen's Outdoor Publishing, Dept. "LOB-8", 2640 Elizabeth Place, Lakeland, FL 33813. They are $14.95 each (postpaid).

▬▬▬ WHERE ELSE CAN YOU OBTAIN MAPS? ▬▬▬

- Local fishing maps are sometimes sold by chambers of commerce.

- Detailed county road maps are sometimes available through state departments of highways and public transportation. County road maps generally are prepared from aerial photos which show details of lake surfaces and rivers.

- Aerial maps containing topographic features can be helpful to fishermen and are available at some airports.

- Blueprint companies, which are usually listed in the yellow pages under "maps", are another source of topographical maps.

CHAPTER 18

PERSONAL FLOAT FISHING
How you can use belly boats to increase the catch

I looked, then looked again. It was an unusual sight to see a man in an innertube fishing in 15 feet of water. He had slowly appeared from behind the brushy islands that dotted the lake in front of my home. I soon realized, however, that he knew what he was doing.

As I continued to watch his activity, his casts centered on some unknown underwater structure. Normally, anglers on the lake concentrate on the waters beneath the overhanging limbs and branches of the islands. This innertube angler was casting towards an open water area away from the structure.

After a few minutes, he heaved backward and water splashed around the buoyant tube. His rod bowed as he battled a respectable-sized largemouth. I watched as he fought the fish to within reach and took a jaw-hold. The angler strung the bass through his waist-stringer.

Watching the action between an innertube angler and a bass was certainly different than the usual bass-to-boat activity. A man in an innertube over deep water will attract attention from those unfamiliar with this productive angling method. But serious fishermen know that a float tube can be a wonderful ally, especially in waters where it's difficult to launch a boat.

Tubing or belly boating, as its often called today, is especially productive in spring and fall, when bass are usually holding tight to structure. It's most enjoyable, though, in the summertime. When most anglers have a hot summer sun pounding down on them and their boat, tubers can feel comfortably cool in their wet surroundings.

Creeks that are narrow and lined with trees may be too small for boat traffic, but not for tubers. The maneuverability of a belly boat makes them ideal for such waters.

Look For Fishing Effectiveness Design Features

The belly boat consists of an inner tube which is partially lined with a cloth material. The covering and seat are usually made of nylon which is rot and mildew resistant. The float tube can be commercially purchased or home-made. Jeans and tennis shoes can be worn, but for more comfort and often productivity, additional gear is recommended.

- Chest-high waders, either stocking foot or boot foot, are usually needed to protect your legs from underwater obstructions.

- Swim fins will more easily propel the craft when you are in water over waist deep.

I put together my first float tube in the mid-fifties. The crude craft was constructed from an old patched up truck tire inner tube and a denim seat covering that my mother had fashioned for me to straddle. A rope tied the whole thing together and allowed for a convenient stringer tie.

I caught many fish from the primitive float. The cloth was heavy when wet, and it soaked up water like a sponge. The material

Larry Larsen on Bass Tactics

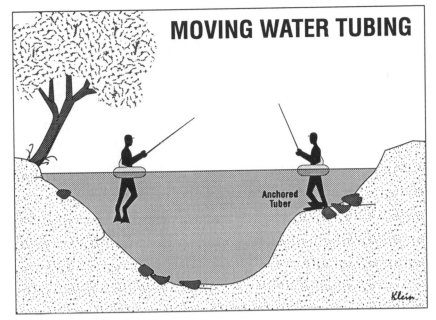

MOVING WATER TUBING

Anchored
Tuber

Rivers and creeks, especially those with cover-laden or steep banks, are perfect locales for the tube angler. Overhanging trees and mild rapids don't seem to bother the float tuber as much as they would a boat angler. When the depths are shallow enough, the tuber can "anchor" quickly simply by standing.

eventually rotted and had to be replaced several times. I also had trouble keeping the tube full of air, but for the most part, my first "boat" was an exciting one.

Today, I would advise you to consider commercially-made coverings for the following reasons:

a. They are lightweight and even have a few pockets in them to hold tackle and essential gear.

b. They don't absorb water and are extremely durable.

c. Sharp sticks and rocks seldom penetrate the tough materials.

d. Belly boats come in several designs and colors with options ranging from carrying straps to backrests.

Personal Float Fishing 117

Control Of The Tube Is The Key To Productivity

The rig may feel awkward at first, as you try to assemble everything that you'll need on the water in a handy place and then to actually fish from one. That feeling will pass quickly if your belly boat is fairly well constructed. The key to selecting one is to make sure that it will support the weight that you intend to put in it (on the seat) and on it.

Learning how to control your craft with swim fins is relatively easy. It'll take a few moments to experiment with your new means of propulsion, but once you learn to kick upward to thrust backward and scissor kick to turn the rig, you won't have any problems.

How To Select The Best Place To "Launch"

A belly boater can "launch" just about anywhere he can step off a shore or wade into water. Successful tube anglers study maps to find ponds, pits, river oxbows or other "hidden" waters that may be appropriate for his type of fishing. Many such places have bass in them that have never seen a lure.

Here's what to look for:

- Small, relatively inaccessible ponds are ideal waters for the tuber.

- Any place without a launch ramp or 4-wheel drive vehicle access is a candidate for a great belly boat expedition.

- Waters far enough away from a road are the remote hotspots that many belly boaters find. Those anglers wanting to transport their john boats across ground to a honey hole will always find the float tube easier to handle. Strap the rig to your back and head out.

- Overgrown farm ponds, those with a brushy perimeter and steep banks, are ideal for such escapades.

Circumventing The Wall Of "Plantdom"

If you have ever fished many such waters without a boat, you will appreciate the access that a tube allows. I once fished several plantation irrigation ponds on Kauai in the Hawaiian Islands, and the bank access was difficult on many. The perimeters of several had a 30-foot strip of eight-foot-high rushes surrounding the water. Such places are the perfect place for a belly-boat because:

a. Any cast would spend the last 30 feet high and dry.

b. Chest-high waders wouldn't have solved the problem due to the depths that the weed line lay in.

c. We couldn't fight our way through the weeds to a casting position in shallow water, let alone on dry land.

d. You don't risk going into the deeper areas over your head, though, with the flotation provided by the tube.

Obviously, without the benefit of a tube or boat, we moved quickly to another plantation pond with a better shoreline for bank-bound anglers.

Large natural lakes and reservoirs are often deep, but relatively shallow and accessible waters exist for the belly boater. Backwater sloughs, sometimes inaccessible to boats, will offer an open door to the tuber.

How To Effectively Work An Area From The Tube

With a belly boat, the fisherman has few limitations regarding the presentation of any lure. Seldom are standard techniques for catching largemouth from a boat not applicable to the tube angler. You can get as close to the quarry as you wish, or as far away. You can position the belly boat wherever you need to in order to correctly "work" an area.

Some caveats exist however:

• You have great stability vertically and even side-to-side (roll), but some lures being retrieved will tend to turn the float tube. It will spin toward the crankbait, as one is bumping along the bottom back to the rod, for example. The plug's resistance in water is greater than the rotational resistance of the float tube on top of the water.

• Setting the hook may require more use of your wrists to be effective. The angler's back tends to rotate backward on a "heavy-duty" hook set and you may end up with some water down your waders. Leaning forward and using your wrists and forearms to set the hook should keep the angler dry and prevent the discomfort of water inside the waders.

• While you'll find it easy to land a fish from the craft; you still have to be aware of the hooks on your bait. That's particularly true when not wearing protective waders on your legs.

You'll probably want to play the fish out, before you land him. Horsing a "green" fish in too quickly can cause anxiety at tubeside. I always take along a small landing net that is just large enough to entrap a 12-pound largemouth swimming headfirst into it. Keep it handy but out of the way, though, until needed. When fishing the spots belly boaters most often are able to get into, that net is usually required very quickly.

Don't Be Afraid To Walk A Marathon To Tube

Back in the early 1960's, I walked half a mile in chest-high waders to tube fish a small creek that wound its way through an overgrown, brushy shoreline in central Kansas. My friend Charles Eby and I carried our inner tubes and tackle into the steep-banked creek and eventually found a way to work down to the stream bed.

From our second or third cast on, the action never stopped. We tossed small spinnerbaits and injured-minnow plugs at a variety of largemouth bass and panfish. Each bend provided overhanging trees and bushes and plenty of strikes. The depth of the creek varied from ankle-deep shoals that we had to hike through to spots that appeared well over 12 or 14 feet deep.

Our trek encompassed only about a mile, but it seemed like five. It took us over four hours to fish that section of the creek, and the time was well spent. We each ended up with 10 chunky bass. The five fish that we put on our stringer and toted out averaged three pounds apiece. Where was the modern "catch-and-release" ethic back then?

The creek in the hilly part of the state may have had a name, but I doubt it. In many sections, the water wasn't even moving, and it was obvious that a two- or three-month-long drought could have wreaked havoc with the fish population.

We had no idea what we would find when we started our jaunt, but when we arrived back at the car we knew three things. First, float tubes were the only possible way someone could fish the water, and second, there were hundreds of bass stacked up in the nondescript waters that no one knew existed. Our final revelation was that never again, and I mean never, would we try to walk a mile out of a remote honey hole with float tube, waders, tackle, and a 15-pound stringer of largemouth each!

Larry Larsen on Bass Tactics

CHAPTER 19
TUBING TECHNIQUES AND CAUTIONS

What to throw, how to throw it and what to look for

For shallow water fishing, tubing is hard to beat. Tube fishing equipment wasn't designed with the goal of covering a lot of water, but it's an excellent way to cover water thoroughly. Here's how to maximize the coverage and the action when fishing from a belly boat.

● Flippin' small jigs and worms - Tubing is a perfect way to flip for bass in tight cover without disturbing the habitat. The tube angler can "dog paddle" in and out of tight spots while flipping a jig or worm into the heavier cover.

● Dead worming - The method of barely moving a plastic wiggler is particularly productive during the spring when the bass seem to get lock-jaw. For the stable float tuber, the method is ideal.

Stability is the key to both methods. Belly boaters sit comfortably in the "hole" of the donut-shaped craft and the water level never tops their chest-high waders. With the lower part of their posterior below the water level, the craft is extremely stable.

A "dead wormer" or "flipper" can slowly fish the bait with the patience and stealth often needed to attract inactive fish. Thanks to the stability, it would take considerable effort to flip one over under any circumstances. Waders employing either method often unsuspectingly step in holes which usually are about two inches above the top of their hip-boot or chest-highs. Tubers don't have the problem, even in muddy waters where the bottom is not visible.

Small Lures, Flies & Low Profiles

Fishing small lures from a personal flotation craft is also particularly effective in clear water. A tube fisherman has a much lower profile than a boat angler. This allows anglers to get closer to the fish-holding habitat, have better lure control and more leverage after the strike.

Fly fishermen love the low profile position offered a tuber. Wind resistance is minimal near the water's surface for their looping casts. The method is well suited for the bass bug-tossers.

Beware of The Creature Hazards

Many potential tubers worry needlessly about snakes, alligators and other denizens. The fact is that they should be respected and avoided if possible, but they are not cause for panic. In fact, you'll probably get used to "close encounters of the wildlife kind."

I'm as afraid of a cottonmouth as anyone, and I'll keep my eyes open for them, but seldom have I been confronted by one. I always avoid being in close quarters with snakes, though. They are more prone to be on shore or in the limbs of trees offshore. That's where you should move carefully.

Most snakes are not aggressive and will go the other way. If one you have sighted doesn't veer off, lean back and kick your swim fins to boil the surface in front of you. If that doesn't work, keep on kicking and propel yourself away from the potential conflict.

Southern-Specific Considerations

I can honestly say that I've seen at least one alligator every day from my office window (Olympian Carl Lewis could long jump to the water) for the past several years and every day while on the water fishing in Florida. They shouldn't cause concern for those who are relatively careful. Here are the facts:

- I've been in the water with alligators on numerous occasions and haven't been pulled under yet.

- During daylight, an alligator will normally keep its distance, but they can be curious.

- Smaller alligators are usually the less-cautious and more curious.

- Although larger ones have been known to grab a duck or small dog, they are seldom aggressive toward large animals (humans).

Exceptions to the above (when you should worry) usually occur at night when they are more actively feeding, in the spring when they are nesting, or with alligators that are being fed by man (and

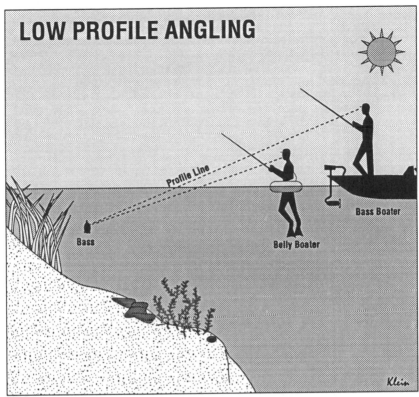

The lower profile of a tuber means that he can get closer to the fish without disturbing them. He will then be able to better control the lure presentation, to set the hook and to fight the fish.

have little hesitation about coming to people). While nesting occurs on land, a protective parent will swim toward an intruder (boater, wader or tuber) in the water.

Don't Take Chances With Thunderstorms

Weather in the form of lightning can be more of a problem than either snakes or gators to the average belly boater. A storm with electricity is something all boaters and even bank fishermen should avoid. It is dangerous even to the low profile angler in a float tube. Graphite and boron rods are excellent conductors (and attractors) of lightning, so leave the water immediately when hearing thunder or seeing bolts of lightning.

Know The Potential Problems Man Can Cause

Another concern of many is having a leak in their innertube as they float over 30 feet of water. Assuming that your equipment is modern, it should be reliable. Air leaks are usually slow and show up in the garage long before they reach the water.

Even if a hook somehow penetrates the tube, it should hold enough air to get back to shore. Leaks under the surface of the water are revealed by a stream of rising air bubbles. Dry rot of the rubber float is seldom a problem for the active tube fisherman if you follow a couple of guidelines.

1. Keep the tube clean and away from oil and grease while in storage for maximum life.

2. Remove the cover periodically to check for foreign objects trapped between it and the tube.

The protective covering usually protects the tube from being penetrated by a sharp limb. Tubes that are not over-inflated, likewise, will be more resistant to puncture. They are more flexible and forgiving around emergent timber or other near-surface structural projections.

Don't Forget Your Safety Vests

It's usually wise anyway for the angler to wear one of the comfortable life vests that are now on the market. Stearns, Coleman, and BassMann make some excellent ones with handy pockets for additional on-the-water tackle storage.

In some states, tubes or belly boats may be considered water craft subject to Coast Guard-approved regulations concerning the wearing of a flotation device. Check with your local regulatory agency.

Although many bass fishermen don't often see the potential advantages of tube angling, other anglers are already thoroughly familiar with this system. Trout fishermen and experienced fly fishermen, in particular, know the value of stealth and low profile approaches. They have been using chest high waders and innertubes successfully for years.

Boats aren't the only way to work offshore structures effectively. Many anglers are turning to belly boats for a most refreshing and exciting way to chase wary largemouth. If you want to check out this means of productive bass fishing, go ahead. You'll be far away from the crowd when you don your personal flotation system on small waters. And, you will enjoy being part of the "wet set," especially on a hot summer day!

CHAPTER 20
HOW TO FISH FORAGE WASHES
Waterfalls and Runoffs Often Run Full...of Bass

To bass, it's an endless food supply. Moving water is a natural attraction to largemouth and most other game fish. Quite a few anglers now concentrate on the advantages of the flow. Locating such conditions and then fishing the currents is becoming increasingly popular.

Food washing into the area is the draw, and the advantages of locating a concentrated group of feeding fish are obvious. The often fat and healthy specimens are uniformly positioned for grabbing the forage morsels, and they are generally shallower than at most other times. While moving water is generally rich in nutrients, it is also usually cooler and more oxygenated.

With the oft times abundant food supply, the fish won't have to expend much energy chasing after smaller members of the food chain. The result is larger fish in such locations. When they have first shot at the supply, they naturally grow faster and bigger.

In unfamiliar water, I'll generally head for any running water that I can find. I know that baitfish are often washed into the mouths of their prey in such areas. Moving water is not always possible to find, but when it is available, you'll probably catch some fish.

You Can Usually Find Bass Around Spillways & Dams

I was recently far south in the Ten Thousand Island area of the Everglades National Park for my first time. The river water was brackish and affected by the tides. The saltwater fish were abundant; redfish, flounder, drum, and small snook were the catch of

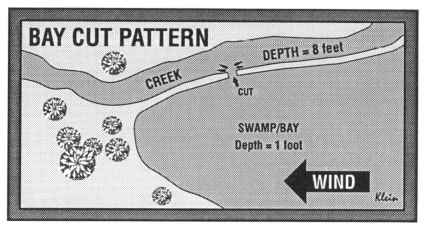

Cuts from swamps or shallow bays are prime bass concentration points due to forage availability. Position your boat in the deep creek or canal and work the edges and mid section of the cut with minnow-imitating lures for top action.

the day for the rest of the outdoor writers that I was with. But I was interested in largemouth bass.

Trying to figure out where the largemouth were was my goal. Without a bigmouth tugging on my line, I'm a little lost. I tried my best to get excited about the salty fish with my compadres, but even after catching several different species, I yearned for a freshwater bass. I had a good idea where I might catch a few, but the spot that turned out to be the best surprised me.

A small dam spread across one of the many tributaries which dumped fresh Conservation Area waters into the finger-like bays of the Gulf of Mexico. The swirling water beneath the concrete structure would hold some largemouth. I knew that.

The water was brackish, but the salinity was low enough for the freshwater bass. I cautiously moved up toward the dam, tossing a Mepp's spinner. My third cast resulted in a smashing strike and a high flying snook.

I released the 17-incher and cast again. I worked the bait near the rocky bottom knowing not only of the possible snags but also of the bass awaiting. A two-pound largemouth struck at it, and after three leaps skyward and a good tussle in the fast current, it was brought aboard to try out the live well. In the following 10 minutes, I caught another two largemouth, a twin to my first snook, and missed a couple of good strikes.

Larry Larsen on Bass Tactics

Largemouth will often lie at the edge of the heavy current in quieter surroundings. Runoff areas where a lake cove necks down providing a current are great places for big largemouth.

Other Unique Strategies May Work As Well

The action below the dam slowed, so I began thinking of how to find some additional bass. The boat was anchored about 30 feet from the dam structure and the bottom became shallower, reaching near the surface in a couple of areas just below the dam. I had thoroughly worked most of the water in the spillway with a variety of lures, and it was time to try something new.

● I noticed some productive-looking cover on the shore just above the dam structure. The surface of the water was about eye-level and I had no idea how deep it was on the other side, but it was worth losing a lure to find out!

● I tossed a Little George as far as I could along the shoreline above the dam. I half-way expected a hang-up before my retrieve had reached the dam, and surely anticipated hooking the top of the dam if the lure got that far.

● I had retrieved the heavy tail-spinner lure about 20 feet when the rod was jolted by the sudden attack of a hungry largemouth. The three-pounder jumped twice before I worked her to the dam.

- The third time I saw her was when I "horsed" her over the dam. She fell six feet down into the white water as I frantically reeled to take up the event's resulting slack.

I gained control of the bass once again and lead her out of the rocks and to the boat. My net helped her into the live well. That's something, I thought; I'd have to try that again. My next three casts were unproductive, but I did get my lure to scoot across the dam without a hang-up. My following cast gained another strike, however, and a two-pound bass was soon tumbling over the dam. The lure was dislodged in the fall, though.

Not to be discouraged, I kept tossing, and in the following hour, caught three more dare-devil bass. My catch from the formidable obstacle was sizable, yet I had only lost one lure in the rocks below the dam and one to a snag above the structure. That loss was worth it.

The ease with which the lure and hooked bass could be brought over the dam was surprising. Even the great angling opportunity that existed for a caster willing to try the spot was, to me, surprising. When 99 percent of the anglers thoroughly fish out the spillway, they leave. I learned to cast above the structure and check it out.

Know The Key Bass Concentrating Factors

In addition to a food source, productive running water areas must also have the important ingredients of depth and cover. Adequate amounts of each is required to hold fish for extended periods. Depth over three feet deep in roily water and some structure should be present nearby for optimal conditions.

Depth is particularly vital to runoff situations. Many pits and strip mines are interconnected via a water control structure and/or large pipe. This typically discharges into an adjacent pool through a large three- or four-foot-diameter pipe, creating a beautiful spot for the run-in.

There is maximum activity when water is moving:

- The discharge is manipulated at times to provide water for continued use in the mining processing operation. A tubular spillway situation exists with moving water bringing in food sucked from the pit above.

- When the water control boards are removed, the free flow through the large pipe structure results in a tremendous discharge below.

- Fish either look for depth to get below the increased current or find heavy cover to hide behind. They will remain in one position, however, to watch for forage washing past.

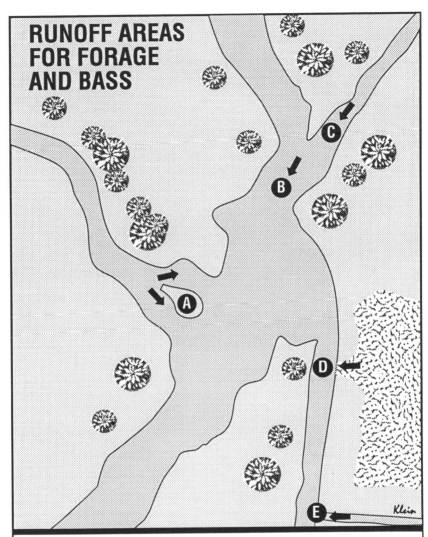

RUNOFF AREAS FOR FORAGE AND BASS

In this figure, an underwater island 'separates' the flow at Location A. At Location B, a major river enters the lake and Location C is the confluence of two tributaries. Location D is a cut from the adjacent marsh and at Location E, a small cut enters a larger one.

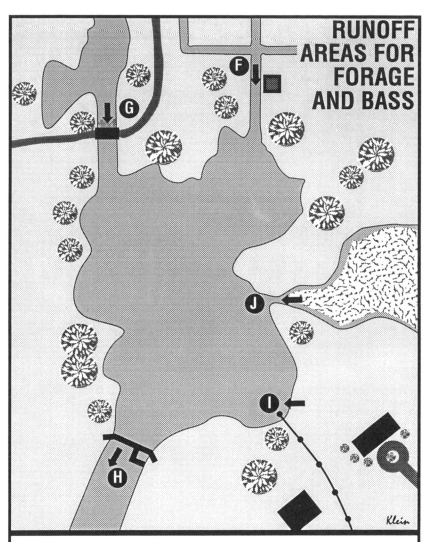

At Location F in the figure above, an irrigation pump house controls flow, and at Location G, a bridge clogged with debris blocks the current. Location H is the spillway below a lock or dam. Location I is a grass runoff, and Location J is the entrance of a swamp or 'wet prarrie'. All runoff situations can provide excellent bass angling.

Check Out All Pipe Discharges

I was tossing crankbaits and worms on the small pit with friend Mike Kennedy. The discharge offered a medium current from the pipe into the long, narrow pit.

We positioned his Gheenoe near the discharge pipe and dropped anchors off each end. Within 10 minutes, we each had a fish and the action remained consistent for the following hour. We had caught 12 fat largemouth when the "discharge tender" came by and removed three more four-inch wide boards from the level control structure.

With the additional flow from the pit above, the current increased and the bass really turned on. I switched to a flutter spoon and counted 10 consecutive strikes by casting into the turbulence and jigging it back toward the boat. I landed eight largemouth and kept half for a stocking project. The lead spoon continued to catch fish, and I had a largemouth on about every other cast for the next 30 minutes.

Not all runoff is perfect. The "discharge tender" again pulled up in his pick-up truck and extracted another dozen boards from the control structure. The water then blew out of the pipe creating a torrent through the area. Our fishing was shut off at the discharge, so we moved downstream past a shallow bar to find the deeper haunts of the largemouth. I knew that they would still be in the area, keeping an eye out for food.

When the discharge intensified, most of the bass moved to a deeper point. That is where we relocated them and caught another eight largemouth before leaving. Very few bass of any significant size were taken this day, but we managed to take two limits of healthy one- to two-pound "stockers" to another lake for release.

CHAPTER 21
FAST-PACED RUNOFF STRATEGIES
Try these presentation tips to take more bass

Runoff situations are fairly typical in many waters found around the country. Bass that live in and around current are in a fast-paced world with definite preferences toward forage, lure presentation, and water characteristics.

Largemouth are normally facing up-current, expecting their forage to wash down toward them. Any forage imitation moving "upstream" against the current will seldom result in a strike.

- The bogus bait appears unnatural to the wary largemouth emphasizing that lure presentation in these situations is critical.

- A lure tossed into fast moving water may be hard to control and the strikes difficult to detect. The protected waters off the main current in the eddies are prime areas to work for largemouth.

- Cast your lure up-current and bring it back across the eddy line. It is at the edge of the fast water where most bass will strike.

A guide friend recently found some big bass in the oxbows just below a dam on a Florida tributary. The hungry largemouth were out of the fast current in the quiet waters on the edge. He and a client caught 14 largemouth including a nine- and an 11-pounder.

Two days later, my friend and I returned to the spot and found the intensity of the water coming over the dam had subsided. The bass hiding out behind the islands and in the oxbows off the main river current were no longer there. They had moved back up beneath the froth at the base of the dam.

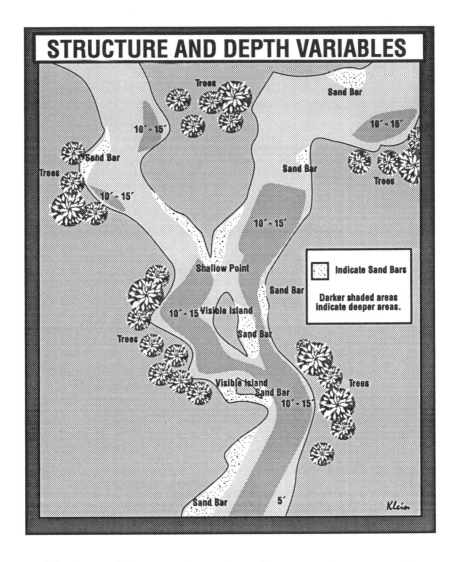

STRUCTURE AND DEPTH VARIABLES

Trees

Sand Bar

10′ - 15′

10′ - 15′

Sand Bar

Trees

Sand Bar

Trees

10′ - 15′

10′ - 15′

Shallow Point

Sand Bar

☐ Indicate Sand Bars

Darker shaded areas
indicate deeper areas.

10′ - 15′ Visible Island

Sand Bar

Trees

Visible Island
Sand Bar

Trees

10′ - 15′

Sand Bar

5′

Klein

We located them and caught well over a dozen on silver crankbaits and spinners, but found nothing larger than three pounds under the dam's spillway.

Here Are The Best Presentations For Current

The best techniques generally depend upon cover available. The lure chosen must be presented properly to assure action, even

INFLOW BASS POSITIONS

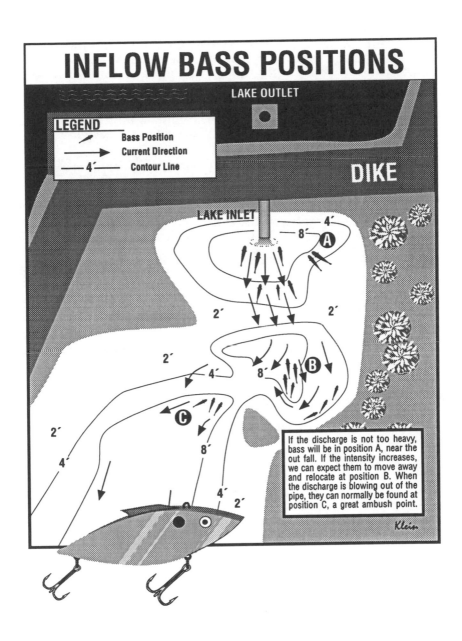

LAKE OUTLET

LEGEND
Bass Position
Current Direction
—4´— Contour Line

DIKE

LAKE INLET

4´
8´
A

2´
2´

2´

8´
B

2´

4´

C

2´

4´

8´

4´
2´

If the discharge is not too heavy, bass will be in position A, near the out fall. If the intensity increases, we can expect them to move away and relocate at position B. When the discharge is blowing out of the pipe, they can normally be found at position C, a great ambush point.

Klein

Fast-Paced Runoff Strategies

135

in fish-laden waters. The current pushing the boat downstream must also be dealt with and the interface between the craft and the bass is vital. Here are some tips on finding the most productive spots.

- In some areas, the only slack water will be right up next to shore or in a deep water pool below the turbulent outflow current. If you drift with the current, you may miss too many potential hot spots.

- Move to the outside of the first bend downstream of the runout of dam tailrace where the current should be strongest. This is where debris and other log jams form, and it is the area that should be fished from the inner bend.

- Find a narrow area where the current speeds up, providing great ambush points for bass just below the neck.

- Look for tributaries which also carry runoff of some sort. Water movement and depth are requirements of the better tributary areas.

- Cast a lure up against any bank with cover in the form of rocks or brush. These areas on the fringe of moving water often hold some big bass.

- Cast any protruding cover in current where the fish may lie behind the force breaker. Bass prefer not to have to continually fight the swift waters and will usually be on the outside edge of a current force.

- Trees and large rocks are great protection from the moving waters where offering the irregular cover for ambush. Bass can position themselves to be cognizant of anything washing down to them and yet have the time to react and eat it!

- Boat control is especially important if moving. A strong trolling motor will aid in precisely controlling the drift, but be prepared for sudden changes in current direction which may sweep a craft into shore.

- Try to position the boat in eddies or out of the current so that control time is minimal.

Watch The Line For More Bass Strikes

A successful angler will be a line watcher in moving water conditions. Due to water turbulence, a careful eye on the monofilament is vital. I normally use Berkley's photochromic

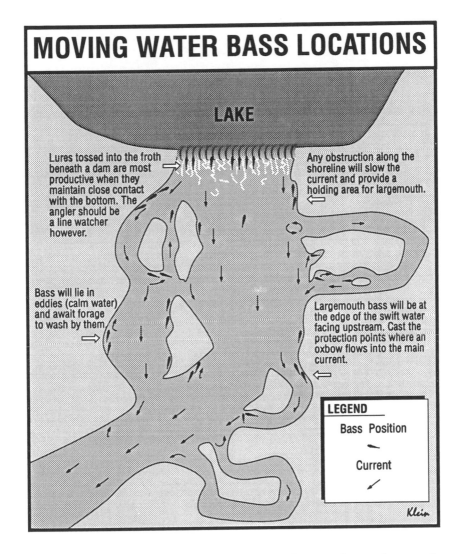

MOVING WATER BASS LOCATIONS

LAKE

Lures tossed into the froth beneath a dam are most productive when they maintain close contact with the bottom. The angler should be a line watcher however.

Any obstruction along the shoreline will slow the current and provide a holding area for largemouth.

Bass will lie in eddies (calm water) and await forage to wash by them.

Largemouth bass will be at the edge of the swift water facing upstream. Cast the protection points where an oxbow flows into the main current.

LEGEND

Bass Position

Current

TriMax which is limp enough for easy casting, yet is tough enough to drag a jigging spoon along a sandy bottom below a discharge pipe.

My line weights vary from 14-pound test up to 20 for normal runoff water situations. Bass in these conditions have little time to spot the line or to detect a counterfeit bait.

Lure selection is, however, very important to the successful angler with aspirations toward a stringer of largemouth.

- Crankbaits are excellent choices for use in moving water and deep-running billed lures in a silver-foil or shad paint job are favorites in such areas. I'll always lean toward a shad or crayfish imitation in these forage-intensive places. Chrome sides and brown crayfish patterns that run three to eight feet down take their share of largemouth cranked from swirling water.

- Jigs are also a favorite of many waterfall anglers. White 1/4 to 3/8 lead heads with white plastic curl tails are commonly chosen attractors. The attrition rate is high when fished along a rocky bottom.

- Jigging spoons can be bounced along the bottom for a good share of the bass market. Again, the lure may just stop, so be prepared to strike back.

- Tail-spinner baits also attract their share of bass in these fishy areas.

- Weedless Texas-rigged worms in a 7- or 8-inch length and colored red shad, pumpkinseed or black grape with silver glitter are productive. Lures that get down quick in the moving water and resemble forage are hard to beat.

To those anglers who haven't experienced the pleasures of catching fish from moving water, I offer this advice: Find the condition and try it; you won't be disappointed.

CHAPTER 22

BOAT HOUSE BATTLES

How to locate productive bass hotels & create a vacancy

Bass are object-oriented fish and that reality couldn't be made clearer than by observing them in the aquatic environment. A scuba diver in relatively clear water can easily note the most attractive bass haunts and how the species utilizes such.

What may be even more significant is the realization that bass hide in the shadows of such structures. The reason for such behavior is two-fold. Bass are predators and seek an advantage in ambush. They are also aware of their own predators, most of which come from above.

To the scuba diver, the difference between visibility in open water versus that in deep shadows is obvious. An all-encompassing shadow from a large overhead structure seems to block out all light. To see into the shadowed area, the diver often has to put his face and mask right into the darkened area. In these situations, eyes must become accustomed to the decreased light levels before being able to "make out" exactly what is lurking in the dark.

Naturally, baitfish under similar circumstances have the same problem - seeing their predators. That fact makes some man-made objects ideal for the largemouth.

- Bass forage is extremely vulnerable in the shadowy maze of a pier or boat house support structure. Clustered pilings beneath a solid platform or sun-blocking roof structures enhance the bass attack position.

For that reason, largemouth can be found concentrated under piers, boat houses, floating docks and pier houses. Not all structures are alike however, and a productive angler is usually the one

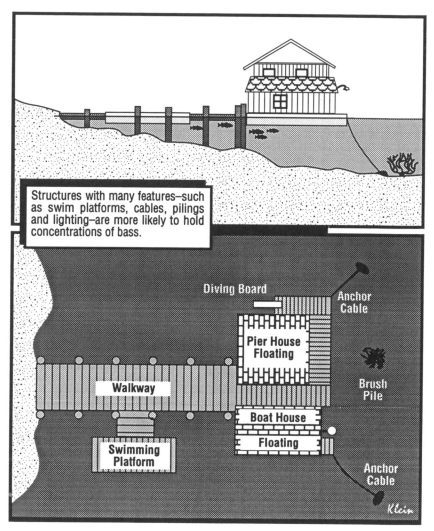

Structures with many features–such as swim platforms, cables, pilings and lighting–are more likely to hold concentrations of bass.

Diving Board

Anchor Cable

Pier House Floating

Brush Pile

Walkway

Boat House

Floating

Swimming Platform

Anchor Cable

Klein

who can quickly "cull" the poorer ones. The architecture of the object is critical for a more productive pier or boat house, as is the presence of forage. But, food and cover are not all there is to the equation.

Other Factors In The Optimal Largemouth Haunt

Depth is also important most times of the year, particularly for the trophy-size bass. Larger fish generally won't venture far from

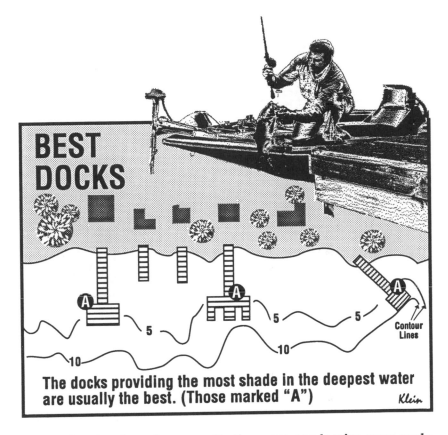

BEST DOCKS

5

5

5

5

10

10

Contour Lines

A

A

A

The docks providing the most shade in the deepest water are usually the best. (Those marked "A")

Klein

protective depths. As a result, the most productive man-made structures are often built on points, outer channel bends and other locations where deep water is near.

Bass will seldom congregate beneath a boathouse or pier on a flat in the back of a shallow cove. A "food shelf", such as a dense grassbed, creek mouth or submerged brush, is a definite requirement for the better bass-holding docks.

- A change in bottom contour along the structure is an ideal situation, but relatively deep water must be adjacent. Largemouth will range from their "wooden home" to hunt forage but won't go far across the shallows.

- If there's minimal deep water cover available, homesteading largemouth are more apt to use dock structures as their primary habitat.

HOW TO PICK THE BEST PILINGS

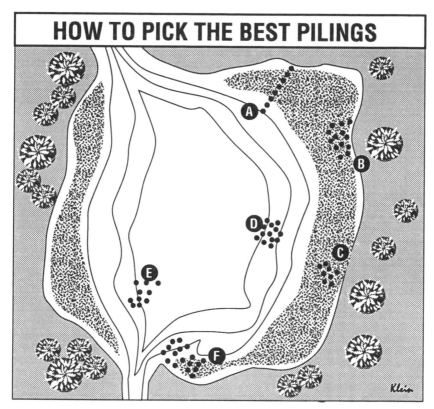

Try to analyze the typical shallow water lake which is studded with heavy grass beds and pilings. Area A is a long fence line running into the lake from shore. This type of breakline is always worth a try, but the size of the fence posts provides less protection to the bass than other pilings in the lake.

Areas B and C are full of pilings scattered in extremely shallow water. There are so many pilings that no unique feature will hold fish in one location. The pilings in area D extend from a mid-depth break to deeper water, a perfect depth zone for big bass under normal water clarity. They are away from the shallow grassline and are a magnet for wayward bass. The numerous pilings are also large (diameter).

Area E is a potentially great fishing location that is near a good dropoff and in deep water. It is close to the river's mouth which is bringing in food in its current. The pilings in area F run right up to the best break in the entire lake, and this area just happens to be at the river's mouth. Grass beds surround the pilings, except on the deep water side which drops off quickly.

Larry Larsen on Bass Tactics

- This is especially true in the summer months. Most natural bodies of water with adequate weed growth on their perimeters are prime waters for attractive wood structures. Deep water options on such lakes and rivers just don't exist for the bass.

- Hot weather and bright sun seem to concentrate largemouth under the better dock structures. Even during mid-day, when bass are supposed to be difficult to catch, a smart angler may hook several from under a productive dock.

- Bass will congregate in areas where they feel safe, and a wide overhead expanse with wood supports is ideal. The more clustered the pilings and the larger the sun blockage, the better. The sun-block in an otherwise bright world is a magnet to largemouth.

- I learned a long time ago that the low platforms which extend closest to deep water generally hold the most fish. They provide more shade and often slightly cooler water temperature. Short, "highrise" docks and piers with several feet between the platform and the water, or those built with planks separated by a large gap, are less utilized by bass. More light infiltrates such places.

DOCK-WALKING

Piers, docks and even platforms with boat houses on their deep-water end are inviting to shore-bound anglers. Bass are accessible to dock-walkers who move quietly and make accurate casts to the productive spots. It's often easy to underhand a bait into the darkness beneath a wide platform.

If the boat house is floating, a productive method is to cast a crankbait past the dock's far corner and then walk to the opposite end prior to beginning the retrieve. The rod is thrust into the water around that corner and the lure's retrieval path then is beneath the boat house foam supports. Naturally, below-water cables could cause hangups.

Non-boaters can also foot-troll a long pier with live bait, as some enterprising anglers have done with success. Giant bass have been caught with this technique using native shiners. Where else but on a man-made structure can the bank angler find access to deeper water and bass-laden cover?

CHAPTER 23

BOAT SHOW "SPECIALS" FOR BASS

Check out marinas and boat houses with these methods

On several occasions, I have discovered big concentrations of largemouth under large, covered boat houses and docks. Over a period of several trips, I've caught three bass over eight pounds and numerous smaller fish from one isolated St. Johns River boat house. There is seemingly a concentration of largemouth present at all times, yet most anglers pass up the cove with a sole boat house. If effectively fished, what a "boat show" the bass there can put on!

Marinas with boat slips divided by low, wood walkway arms can be a gold mine if the timing is right. Such places with high summer traffic are usually more productive early in the day before human activity gets "geared up," or during the fall and spring months.

- Seasonally, the low to normal water levels found in the late summer and early fall are more conducive for docks to hold bass.

Perhaps surprisingly, boat houses and piers are productive after the sun sets. A couple of tips are worthy of note when fishing after dark.

- A full moon provides a lot of illumination and the shadows beneath the platform are still significant.

- The sides of the giant-size boat houses become a factor in the bass predation. Forage between the largemouth and the side of a house on the end of a pier are "dead meat." They stand out.

Lights at night, whether natural or artificial, enhance bass opportunities.

DOCK SUPPLEMENTS

Check out the area adjacent to the ends of docks and piers for additional forage attention.

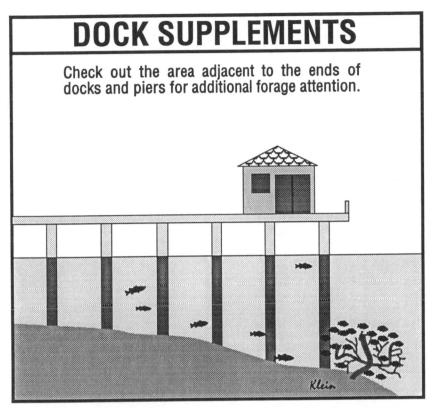

Check Out The Brush Sweeteners Below The Structure

Many lakeside residents "plant" brush or Christmas trees either beneath their docks and piers or within a short cast from the structure. This brush, often supplemented with feed pellets to draw small forage, is usually placed beneath the fishing platforms to congregate crappie. They also interest largemouth for the same reasons.

There are several ways to find this added "attraction" and here are some of the observation keys:

1. Rod holders

2. Flood lights

3. Fishing chairs

4. Tree limbs

5. Hanging ropes or wires

Each of the above may denote regular activity and possibly the presence of an attractor. An enterprising angler may use his depthfinder to locate outlying brush "plantings."

Organic Growth Attracts Forage & Bass

Wood in the form of the brush "sweetener", or the supports themselves, encourage organic growth. Barnacles in tidal-influenced waters and algae in fresh water quickly attach to pilings, initiating the food chain. Less rapid growth occurs on concrete or metal supports.

Algae buildup occurs on the foam supporting floating boat houses and that attracts minnows and the like. Largemouth will often suspend under such table fare. Although fish may get used to constant marina traffic which may dislodge small crustacean,the more stable platforms less used by humans generally make better bass homes.

Casting Accuracy Is The Key To Productive Dock Fishing

Another factor involved with floating structures is the anchor and tie-down cables which seem to get in the way of a perfect retrieve. Such obstacles actually make the dock a better one to fish. Novice casters aren't able to effectively fish platforms with ladders, lights, carpet pieces, canepoles, dangling boat-hoist straps and other temporary or permanent customized features that make the structure irregular. A good caster can.

- Casting accuracy is essential to successful dock fishing because those irregularities, along with the projecting nails and splinters and gaps between planks, can often stop a retrieve or interrupt the perfect cast.

- The fisherman with sharp casting skills and knowledge of the optimal bass locations within or under the dock or boat house will often catch bass from a structure that has just been fished by other, less-effective anglers.

To successfully fish a large dock, the angler must carefully work the structure. Unproductive fishermen may make just one or two casts to the sides and to the front of the platform. Patient anglers, though, may fish it for 20 minutes before catching several.

Few fishermen can cast accurately 50 feet into pockets and gaps of a few inches, and that's where the bass are located. Close-up angling is required for attracting the larger, less active bass that

Docks and boat houses come in all shapes and sizes. The better bass territory lies beneath the ones that throw the largest shadow near deep water. Wooden pilings and support structures with adequate algae growth attract the remainder of the food chain. Predator bass seldom venture far from the shadows to chase a meal.

frequent docks and boat houses. The big ones, territorial as they are, select the prime spots beneath such structures. And those places are the most difficult to reach with a lure.

Accurate Tosses May Depend On The Individual & His Equipment

Short, accurate casts are normally required to place a bait in front of the bass. Successful anglers have mastered flippin', side-arm, backhand and skippin' casting techniques. Their rods are either of flippin' length, 6 1/2 to 7 feet, or short spinning staffs with muscle.

Wind and water conditions affect the presentations around boat houses and docks. A wind blowing right into a boat house causing it to gently roll a little is ideal. The normally inactive dock bass are motivated to be on the lookout for forage. Stained water allows an angler to effectively fish the structure.

Stout line is recommended since only 15 feet or so is in play at any one time, exposed to the perils of the support structures beneath the platform.

- Most seasoned dock anglers use 14- to 20-pound test monofilament in fresh waters and up to 25 in brackish water where razor-sharp barnacles can be a significant problem.

Select The Lures That Will Do The Job

The most effective lures for fixed structures are plastic worms which can be precisely placed. They make little noise on entry into the bass world, can be effectively worked in a small area, and seldom hangup in a clustered maze of support pilings. A lightly-weighted Texas-rigged worm is easily worked in the right areas. Those with soft bodies and arms, like the crayfish versions, can provide maximum motion with minimum movement.

A jig and plastic eel is another good bet for the tight action found beneath a platform. Trailers of pork or plastic can enhance the attraction at times. A jig or worm skipped well underneath the dock may entice the inactive bass.

The retrieve and hook set must be sidearmed or underhanded to avoid a confrontation with the overhead tangles. Pinpointed casting into all conceivable spots and careful thought about the hook set are usually required for dock-hugging largemouth.

When fish from the dark side become active, topwater lures worked alongside the emergent wooden structure may attract bass. Crankbaits then have a place in the presentation. Fish them so that they bounce off all wooden supports. That will trigger the strikes.

Know The Seasonal Variation For Bass Positioning

The position of the bass will also vary depending on the season. Spring will often find largemouth holding on the outer support posts near the shallow food and spawning shelves. During the summer, the bass may position themselves deeper beneath the platform and then when fall arrives, move nearer the internal support pilings.

Rainy weather and overcast skies will allow bass to move near the perimeter supports and off to adjacent brush or vegetation. Regardless of the conditions or time of year, the largemouth that hide under docks, platforms and boat houses can be caught. Successful anglers provide "pier pressure".

Larry Larsen on Bass Tactics

CHAPTER 24

DEALING WITH ADVERSE WEATHER

How to catch bass under tough seasonal conditions

Weather influences often affect the metabolism of bass and their interest in feeding or striking at a lure or bait. Seasonally, most anglers have trouble getting cold water bass to bite. After a cold front, many fishermen simply throw in the towel.

In the spring, the pre-spawning bass pose significant problems to shallow water anglers, and a few months later, the dog-days of summer seemingly make active bass disappear. Most anglers have a number of excuses why fish don't bite, and many are based on the weather.

Let's take a close look at some of the seasonal problems associated with weather and its influence on bass. Maybe you won't need as many excuses this coming year.

You Can Solve Winter Lock-Jaw

The chills of winter have been said to shut down bass activity. Largemouth still feed, although it may be only once every two weeks in the harshest environment. Seemingly dormant, their metabolism has slowed significantly and they typically relocate.

As waters cool with the influx of winter, bass move slightly deeper to warmer waters, and they forage only occasionally. They become acclimated easily to the new depths, but some anglers seem to forget that the fall bass haunts are mostly empty during the winter months.

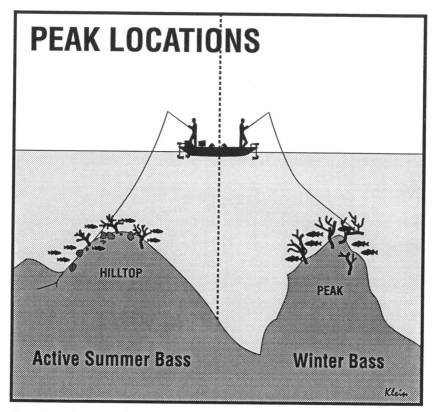

PEAK LOCATIONS

HILLTOP

PEAK

Active Summer Bass

Winter Bass

Klein

Peak locations vary from summer to winter. During colder weather, bass are more apt to be on sharper dropoffs. Summer bass are found on lesser gradients due to more stable water conditions.

You Can Find Winter Bass In The Right Places

• During cold weather, largemouth position themselves on sharp drop offs adjacent to even deeper water. They want to be able to access the depths quickly if an extremely harsh cold front comes through. They take up residence along break lines off bluffs, river banks, points and other steep topography.

• Winter bass concentrations also hold tightly to deep water humps or mounds. They can often be found along channel bends of submerged river beds, particularly those with some structure such as brush or rocks.

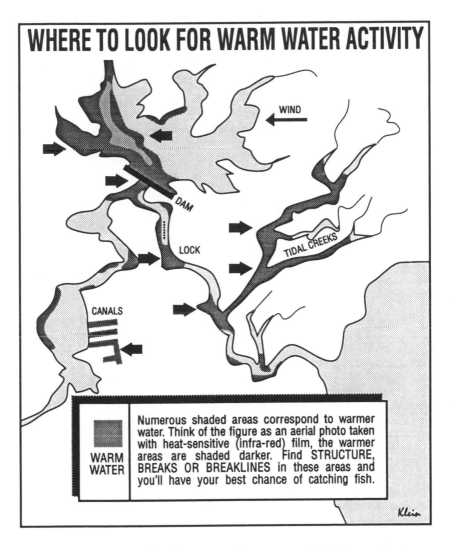

WHERE TO LOOK FOR WARM WATER ACTIVITY

WIND

DAM

LOCK

TIDAL CREEKS

CANALS

WARM WATER

Numerous shaded areas correspond to warmer water. Think of the figure as an aerial photo taken with heat-sensitive (infra-red) film, the warmer areas are shaded darker. Find STRUCTURE, BREAKS OR BREAKLINES in these areas and you'll have your best chance of catching fish.

Klein

Pin-pointing such places requires a good LCG or chart recorder to identify bass which will be holding tight to cover in cold waters. Winter largemouth that are just inches off the bottom may not show up on some sonar units.

Once you have located the most promising structure, the most productive deep water baits that can be fished extremely slow, are

Dealing With Adverse Weather   153

jigging spoons, jig-and-eels and plastic baits. Small movements of the fare along the bottom structures are attractive to frigid largemouth. Bass forage has diminished some, and what is left has a slower metabolism, similar to that of the predator's.

Plan Your Frontal Response Prior To The Event

Cold fronts have an almost devastating effect on the activity of bass. The majority of the fish seem to shut down their "systems", but a few will remain neutral or even active. Finding those bass which are less affected by the front is the key to catching them.

All fronts are not created equal. They affect different bass species in different ways (due heavily to environmental parameters) and even the same species differently in different waters. Here are some general guidelines:

- Severe fronts seem to affect clear water largemouth more than those in muddy water.

- Fronts affect largemouth more than they do smallmouth or spotted bass.

- Fronts affect shallow water fish more than those in deep waters.

- Fronts seem to affect lake bass more than river bass.

To improve your chances of catching bass, simply look over the above list and eliminate the ones affected the most by fronts.

How You Can Even Catch Suspended Bass

Lake bass tend to suspend off points and out over deeper water with the passage of a front. An LCG sonar can sometimes detect bass suspended away from cover, and catching them may be tough. One way to locate "catchable" fish then is as follows:

1. To locate the more active bass - first identify the depth at which suspended fish are positioned.

2. Then move to the nearest structure lying at that very same depth. Often, more aggressive bass will be holding on the structure.

The same plan of action is effective at the time of year when a school of baitfish has been found suspended over deep water. The angler moving to the nearest sloping habitat at that same depth may find predator fish willing to bite.

Larry Larsen on Bass Tactics

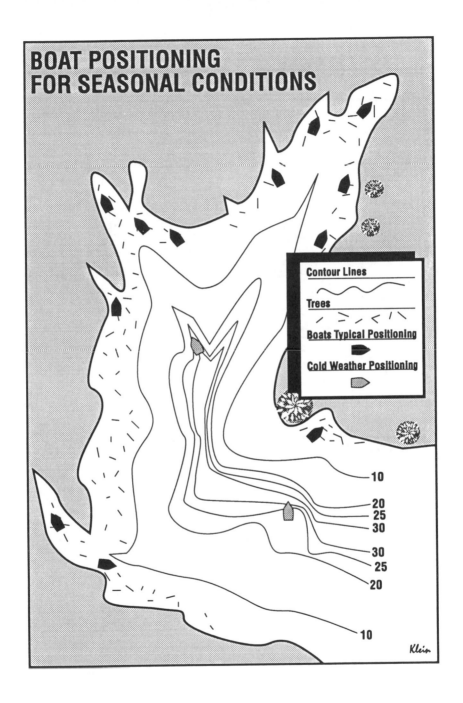

BOAT POSITIONING FOR SEASONAL CONDITIONS

Contour Lines

Trees

Boats Typical Positioning

Cold Weather Positioning

10

20
25
30

30
25
20

10

Klein

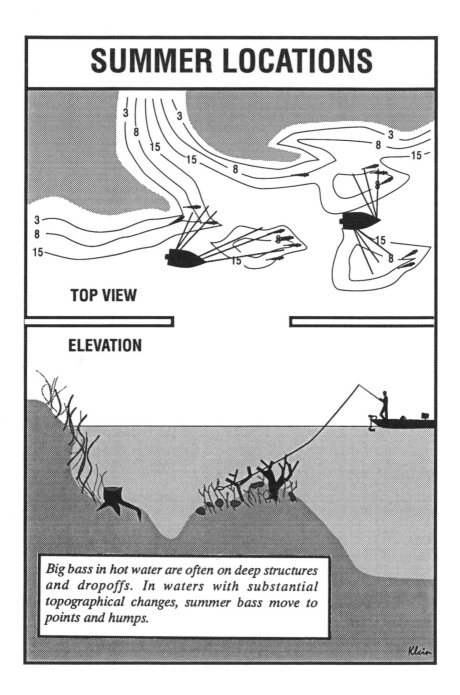

SUMMER LOCATIONS

TOP VIEW

ELEVATION

Big bass in hot water are often on deep structures and dropoffs. In waters with substantial topographical changes, summer bass move to points and humps.

Larry Larsen on Bass Tactics

A productive presentation for frontal-affected bass is again slow, unexaggerated movements.

- Lures that stay close to the concentrations of bass are usually the most successful.

- Small, natural-action type baits attract strikes then.

- Live baits placed in a school of bass or right on structure holding them are often preferred by those of us having to fish in such conditions.

Focus On Catching Spring's Pre-Spawn Bass

In early spring, bass are interested in one thing: spawning, but they do feed and even concentrate in great numbers. Catching them at that time is often related more to finding them than to presenting a precise lure in the exact way.

- Knowing where the pre-spawners "stage" or hold up prior to going on their beds is the key to catching fish in the spring.

Male and female bass will move en masse from the depths when the water temperatures crank up into the mid 60's. They join others just off the spawning flats or coves in "staging areas", and finding concentrations there can make an angler's day. Here's where to look:

- Most staging locations lie in fairly shallow waters, about two or three times deeper than their ultimate beds will be located.

- Generally, staging areas lie along creek channels or off points at the first major breakline out from the spawning grounds.

Finding them is relatively easy with the aid of your sonar unit. Locate the boat adjacent to shallows known to be an annual spawning area, and move toward the deepest nearby water. Mark the first drop-off or creek channel with buoy markers. Lures that reach that depth will usually entice the bass there.

How To Put Excitement Into The Summer Doldrums

Hot weather fish are usually just overlooked. Many are on deep structures that anglers seldom venture to. The situation is not conducive to success for those fishermen who are still sticking with their spring patterns. The shallows are still harboring numerous small bass, but the trophy-size fish are off the beds and have retreated to their deep water haunts.

In natural lakes, the larger bass move out of the grassy flats to take up positions on the edges of weedlines and in depressions on the bottom away from the vegetated shallows. They'll move in shallower to the more intensive food shelves once or twice a day, but finding them the other 22 hours usually requires using the sonar unit. Here's what to do:

- Look for reservoir fish to take up positions in deep waters on humps and along points, not far from forage.

- Throw lures that dredge the bottom or crawl at depths of 8 to 25 feet of water. They'll usually draw strikes from largemouth.

- Select deep-running crankbaits, Texas-rigged worms with 1/2- to 3/4-ounce bullet weights and trolled artificials which can be especially productive for heat wave bass.

CHAPTER 25

INACTIVE BASS FACTORS & TURN-ONS

Understanding environmental and forage influence can mean more bass

Inactive bass are usually the most difficult to catch. Reasons for their adversity vary, but they can be caught. Moreover, not all bass are inactive at the same time. Environmentally, water chemistry characteristics and the available forage have an impact on the activity of bass. In fact, those considerations may greatly influence the activity of bass and their movements.

Anglers are often bewildered about the reasons bass are not feeding under conditions that appear favorable for such. At times, the activity rate of bass may be responsible, while at others, the concentrations of bass may have relocated due to influences in their environment.

Dense habitat in some lakes pose significant problems to bassmen, even though bass may be numerous on a per-acre basis. Potential reasons for not catching bass are numerous, but somewhere, under almost any conditions, largemouth can be enticed to bite a lure.

Handling adverse bass is seldom easy. Here's what seems to work best:

- An understanding of the potential causes of their inactivity or disappearance is vital to formulating a game plan and solving the problem of catching them.

- After that, locating the most active fish is important.

- Then of course, selection and presentation of the bait is the final step to success.

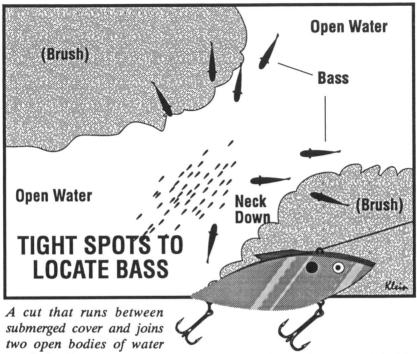

A cut that runs between submerged cover and joins two open bodies of water regularly offers bass an exceptional dining experience. Largemouth lurk in the cover and wait for shad to follow the current through. When predator and prey clash, a vibrating bait is the angler's best ticket.

How To Understand The Water Chemistry Impact

Water chemistry factors cause bass to relocate, so knowing a bit about them will enable an angler to adapt to such changes and catch more fish. Water temperatures that lie between 65 and 85 degrees are usually considered an optimal range for active bass that will eagerly hit lures. Several sonar units on the market offer a built-in surface temperature meter which can be used to track thermal changes. The Lake Systems Combo-C-Lector offers com-

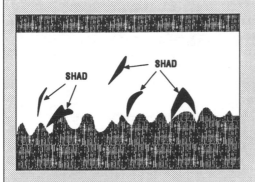

Figure 1 - The mass of threadfin shad are lying low on this typical cold fall day, with few isolated fish braving the cooler surface waters to feed. The temperature-sensitive schools of bass forage are content to remain in the deep, warmer waters of this heated reservoir (via power plant). Bass seem to be unconcerned about feeding in this deeper water during cool early morning hours.

Figure 2 - About mid-morning as the surface waters begin to warm, some of the shad begin to move up to feed on surface or near surface plankton. A few bass begin to get active, but the best is yet to come.

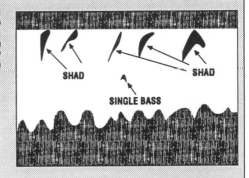

Figure 3 - As the top layer of water begins to warm around midday, most of the shad are feeding near the surface. Largemouth seeking the shad are holding just below them. The bass will move up and down at will until they're stuffed. The forage will remain near the surface.

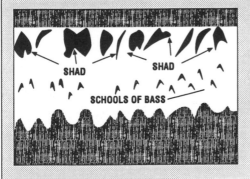

Klein

plete water temperature data from the surface to the bottom. Oxygen and pH values also dictate where fish may be.

- Dissolved oxygen above 6 parts per million (ppm) is conducive to bass health, and if you don't have a meter to check that value, look for evidence of rough fish, like gar, on or near the surface. That reveals bass may have vacated the area.

- Values of pH between 7.0 and 8.5 are usually ideal for largemouth bass and a Combo-C-Lector can identify such for you. Bass are usually in waters offering the closest values to the mid-range above. Extremely low pH values will cause fish to seek more comfortable waters.

For those avid anglers with a greater interest in water chemistry parameters and how they affect bass movement and catches, I will refer you to my book, "Bass Fishing Facts" which goes into great detail on the subject. Book 6 in my BASS SERIES LIBRARY covers Feeding motivations, Predator striking insight, Environmental factors and chapters on the bass senses and behavior during pre- and post-spawn times. Ordering information on this great reference source can be found at the back of this book.

Don't Forget The Very Important Forage Influence

Available forage is a prime consideration to locate and catch adverse bass. Like humans, bass are usually interested in having access to their food.

Knowing the whereabouts of the most prevalent forage in a body of water is the key to locating bass. There are two ways to understand the forage on a given body of water at a given time of year:

1. The best is through careful observation. You may see schools of bait moving along the surface or in the shallows. You may see remains of forage that bass cough up when being landed or in the livewell.

2. A good sonar unit (chart recorder or LCG) can identify schools of forage roaming the open water, as well as pick up the fish arches below them. Use the electronics to find shiners, shad or other baitfish, and you'll usually find the bass.

The Habitat-Intensive Factors Affect Bass Movement

When the water is absolutely loaded with bass habitat, anglers often wonder where to begin their search. Many can't "see the forest for the trees." Bass concentrations may be numerous in such

When most bass are sluggish, the only strike you may get will be a big one. They don't seem to play by the rules. Knowing the right tree type also may be the difference between several and just one or two.

areas, but few anglers will find them. The productive fishermen will key in on certain factors that lead them to the fish. Once located, those bass will strike a lure.

An area inundated with flooded trees may look the same throughout. A bass won't be beside every tree unfortunately, so it requires some thought to determine those spots with the most promise, those areas where numerous bass may be active and ready to hit a lure.

Experience on the water has taught me to look for surface clues in natural waters, such as:

- Taller hardwoods and dark green plant life which usually denote fertile, sandy bottoms.

- Smaller, light green trees along a shore often grow in a shallow, swampy area. It's the fertile bottoms and growth there that correspond to a healthy food chain, right up to the predator bass.

How To Analyze Abundant Habitat In The Impoundments

In the impoundments, after a lake bed is flooded, trees that were left uncut for fish habitat reveal a lot about the topography below. By analyzing those types of cover and then fine-tuning your suspicions with a depth finder, you can tailor your fishing technique for each.

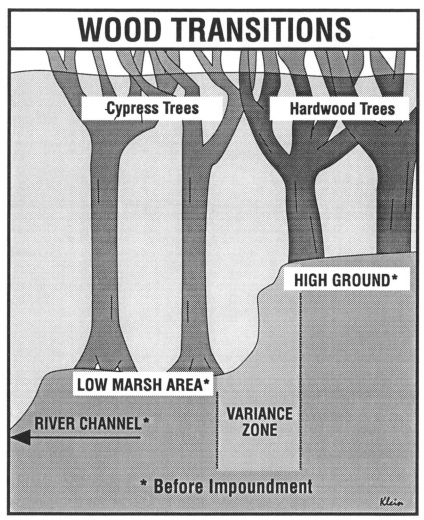

WOOD TRANSITIONS

Cypress Trees

Hardwood Trees

HIGH GROUND*

LOW MARSH AREA*

VARIANCE
ZONE

RIVER CHANNEL*

* Before Impoundment

Learning to identify the woods emerging from a lake can lead to more bass catches. The optimal lures and technique will vary from flooded softwoods to hardwoods.

- Softwoods, like pine trees, will normally be on a flat without a depth break, while hardwoods, like oak and maple trees, usually grow on the edges of old sloughs or ditches.

- The hardwoods are productive year around, with fall and pre-spawn spring being the prime times.

- During the spawn and in the summer, fish the softwoods, particularly in the early morning when bass are moving out of sloughs to feed in the flats.

Learn To Identify The Types of Trees For More Bass

Identifying the woods emerging from the lake is fairly easy. Size of the trees is one indicator, as hardwoods are generally much larger in diameter. Hardwoods also last a lot longer, so forests remain more dense. A stand of softwoods won't be as thick, since they deteriorate much quicker, often in just a few years. Any time something in the water is decomposing, oxygen is also being depleted and that area is seldom ideal for bass.

- Trees light in color, such as those with a soft brown tint, are softwoods, while hardwoods normally turn extremely dark or even black in the water.

- Generally, the further back into a creek that you go, the more hardwoods you'll find.

- To find the most productive spots in the hardwoods, most anglers employ their LCG to find a creek channel or ditch bend within the trees. Fish arches may show on any elevation change on those edges.

How To Entice Bass From Abundant Tree Cover

Once those cover-intensive bass are located, many anglers prefer to toss a crankbait. Great springtime action in the woods can also be had by flippin' worms along the larger stumps on the edge of the creek banks. If the bass are located in trees near a bank, use a buzz bait or top water chugger-type bait.

In the summer, the better wood angling lies in the deeper creek channels near the main lake body. Tree lines denote areas with the presence of deeper water, possible submerged roadbeds or ditches, creek channels, etc., and your sonar unit will locate the exact structure to fish below.

Trees, whether in a natural lake or partially submerged in a reservoir, grow in particular places for a reason. Their spread and uniformity may vary, and so then will the bass fishing.

Larry Larsen on Bass Tactics

CHAPTER 26

BEATING THE CROWDS TO LARGEMOUTH

Try these successful techniques for catching bass from pressured waters

Ever arrive at a secret fishing spot to find another 15 boats have beaten you there? That happens more frequently today than ever before. The problem with such heavy fishing pressure is two-fold. First, the bass are spooky from the constant bombardment of lures and steady boat traffic, and second, they may not be eager to feed, instead taking up residence in the thickest cover for protection. That makes them twice as hard to get to and make them bite.

A line of boats stretching across the parking lot at the public ramp on your state's most popular lake shouldn't scare you off. Neither should the jet boats, jet skiers, cruisers, water skiers and sail boats.

Under the surface that is being whipped to a froth by the onslaught of water craft, swim bass which can be caught. You probably won't catch many, however, by joining the melee and casting with the crowd.

Increased pressure on the bass fishery is due to increasingly proficient anglers having more leisure time, better fishing equipment and more knowledge. More boats and greater interest in fishing is also a reality, one we should learn to accommodate.

There will be room for everyone, but anglers may be relegated to using their heads more often, becoming "thinking anglers." We will be battling crowds for years to come. The chances of a peaceful day on some waters will, unfortunately, remain minimal.

Why Are Some Waters In Favor With Users?

Waters near major population centers are often pounded by hoards of anglers. Waters with a "potential record" reputation attract enthusiastic anglers like a magnet. Even small, but highly promoted and publicized waters are often inundated with visiting fishermen.

When do such waters become out of favor with the anglers? That normally requires the passage of much time and occurrence of many fruitless fishing trips to those waters.

Tournament And Guide Crowds To Avoid

Professional tournament anglers touring the country's lakes are often faced with the challenges of catching bass in a crowd. Competing with 300 or 400 other fishermen for a top prize and, in many cases, the same fishing spots, can be frustrating without a game plan to overcome adversity.

Adding to the crowd of the other contestants are often numerous "locals" who want to follow some of the big name pros and fish where they do. In fact, these tournament contestants will often return to their previous day's best spot to find several competitors' boats and a few local boats occupying the "hole".

There are options other than shouting and fisticuffs. As an observer in a BassMaster's Classic a few years back, I watched as one tournament contender invited the burly Texas pro in my boat to the bank after the weigh-in, because he had felt crowded in a small cove off the Arkansas River. Other than some yelling across the water, no excitement followed. Neither contestant pulled too near the other for the remainder of that day.

Successful guides are also aware of increased activity around them, once their reputation has spread. Most professional guides and tournament bass anglers understand that crowds are a part of the game, though. They adapt and catch fish, or they don't. The successful fishermen usually have a plan of action that works for them.

How Pressure Affects Bass Behavior

Bass normally feed along the edges of habitat, whether under, over or beside such a mass. They feel secure while actively foraging.

- When fishing or boating pressure makes them wary, they will scatter and, if heavy cover is present, move tighter to it.

- Locating subtle places and using slower, more subtle presentations can then become vital to success.

Larry Larsen on Bass Tactics

CREATE YOUR OWN TIRE REEF

One way to avoid heavily-pressured areas is to create your own prime spot in an unpressured area. Tire reefs last seemingly forever and attract forage and bass within a few days after being submerged.

Places that may not be too obvious to the masses can be hot spots. Here are a couple of requirements:

1. The spot must have adequate habitat quality to appeal to the bass, yet not be as visible as others to most anglers.

2. These less obvious spots may be deeper requiring sonar to locate the structure and fish.

Forget the obvious structure, along the shoreline. The shallows take a beating from the crowds on most lakes, and deep structure usually receives less pressure. Often, the best structures are those not shown on maps.

ENHANCE THE DEPTHS WITH TREE STRUCTURE

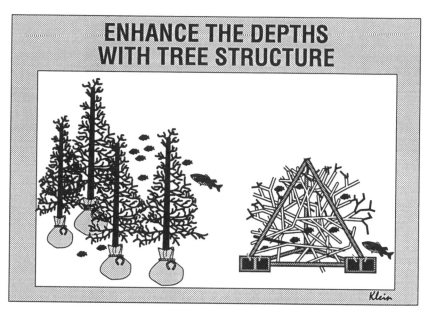

Most visible structure will draw the attention of the "weekend navy." To concentrate bass for your personal angling pleasure, sink wood structures in the depths. While others are flogging the visible trees, you can be catching fish from those secret submerged spots.

One way to combat the crowds is to create your own "low-boat-traffic" fishing opportunities. Offshore structures can be planted, but the secret spot can be exposed, and the crowds will simply move in with you.

• Some anglers sink their own brush piles in the depths far away from the bank, carefully note the location and return to fish it when boats aren't zipping back and forth. Once you have a "honey hole" located, be very close-mouthed about it.

How To Lure Reluctant Largemouth

Bottom bumping lures may be most productive because pressured bass often go right to the bottom and move into heavy cover. The optimal baits then should be something that won't further trigger bass to be jumpy. Thus, smaller lures are often best.

Patience, accurate casts, lighter line and an extra dose of fish attractant may also be keys to success on pressured waters. One approach is to use fish attractant on your lures more often on the weekend days when the masses are competing with you. The same amount of attractant should last five times as long if you relegate your fishing to what are normally called "work days" (Monday through Friday).

Forget Flogging Every Visible Piece Of Structure

The "weekend navy", in its relentless pursuit of America's most popular gamefish, has probably already hit that spot. If a spot has been pounded, it is wise to let it rest, even if the fish have been released. Fish "sore-mouthed" by others may not be aggressive for quite awhile.

More attention to detail is in order when trying to catch pressured bass.

- Slower presentations for spooked fish means line watching is more critical.

- Bites are softer and slower, so the angler has to pay attention to the presentation. Lures that move a few inches at a time catch fish, but the angler must be particularly observant.

- To fish slower and more thoroughly requires extra patience.

When a smart angler enters an area that is covered with boats, the first thing he should do is slow down his presentation and boat movement. Especially in a crowded situation, fishermen have a tendency to move very quickly, and as a result, fish over the top of a lot of bass.

Slow Your Presentation Down To Catch Bass Behind Other Boats

In a competition, the contestants will want to beat the crowd to all areas, and as a result, cover the water too quickly. In a recent major tournament, a few areas drew crowds of contestants. Heavy winds on the main body of the lake pushed many into a cove where one professional had located bass in the practice round.

While in the crowd, the pro employed a lighter line and smaller 4-inch tube lure. He fished behind other boats, but fished the area very methodically, trying to finesse the strikes. Other contestants would move into the cove and quickly fish the bank and leave. The one thing you can count on is that after the first boat passes through such an area, the aggressive or easily-fooled bass are caught.

The pro continued to intensely work the same area, though. He did so with an extremely slow retrieve and ultimately caught several bass over the three-day event. He finished as the winner!

CHAPTER 27

ESCAPE THE PRESSURE
Here are places to go to find bass that the masses can't

In heavily-pressured waters, don't be afraid to take your boat back into the heaviest cover to escape the crowds. When there is little cover nearby, it is wise to try something different from the rest of the crowd. For example, one professional tournament angler tosses a jerkbait anytime he is in a crowded fishing situation. He feels that the jerkbait will attract different, less-pressured fish. The fish may suspend with little cover nearby, or they may just react differently to other types of lures.

If you fish a lure that is different from those everyone else is throwing, you may do better, because the crowd is fishing for the same fish. If everyone is fishing the same type of bait through the same habitat, they may be missing fish that can be caught on a different lure.

- Fishing pressure can cause poor fishing, possibly because the bass react to it by changing their behavior patterns. We are used to blaming the poor fishing on cold fronts, muddy water or other weather factors, but seldom do we acknowledge that fishing or boating pressure may be the culprit.

- Fishery studies have noted that such pressure does indeed affect fish behavior and, correspondingly, fishing success. The predator and its forage even position themselves differently when over-pressured.

On crowded waters, use of live baits may offer some advantages over artificials. The primary advantage is that they will less likely spook a wary bass. They can also be fished in a "strike zone" for a long time with minimal movement. Shiners, for example, can be

Escape The Pressure   173

fished in and around the densest cover. Their use also allows you to easily "camp out" on and thoroughly work a spot in a highly-pressured lake.

Why Jostle With The Crowds? Bass Don't

Waters on weekends or holidays, especially those during the spring or summer months, are always more crowded than they are during the week.

- Take a vacation day or a "sick" day (you didn't hear that from me) and visit the highly-pressured waters on a weekday. Let the Saturday and Sunday crowd have the lake, and let it rest on Monday. Bass have probably seen thousands of lures sailing over their head on the weekend, so you'll probably catch more fish on Tuesday through Thursday.

- Try to avoid jostling with the crowds on the heavy-pressured lakes also by fishing after dark. Even Sunday night is better than during the daylight hours. Water skiers and speed boaters are sunburned by then and the bank-pluggers are tired of casting with little success. Launch your boat when others are taking theirs out. Focus particularly on those bass along the shoreline; they are less wary and are subject to being caught.

- Water skiers and pleasure cruisers start arriving at a lake about 10:30 a.m. and most anglers have arrived by 7:30 a.m., so to avoid the masses either get up early or stay up late. When on the water under the moonlight, you are able to fish closer to the marina or launch ramp or shallower with success. Without hundreds of boats surrounding you, it is much easier to "sneak up" on the bass.

Boat Traffic Can Be An Influence On The Fish...Or Not

If the boat traffic is constant, then it may not provide too much of a problem to anglers. In fact, boats moving by an area may stir up baitfish, which in turn, may activate the bass. Tossing a Rat-L-Trap or fast-moving crankbait may be the most effective way to catch the feeding bass and take advantage of the traffic. On such waters, when things settle down a bit, the bass seem to become inactive again in such situations.

Many experienced anglers recall a time when water ski or pleasure boat activity seemed to turn on the bass. When a ski boat blasts by, a school of bass may move to the surface and feed. After the skier moves by, cast out past the wake and hang on to the rod. Once you get a strike on a couple of consecutive tosses, you'll be looking for skiers to swing past the boat.

Larry Larsen on Bass Tactics

PRESSURED BASS

The Author Recommends:
1 - Throw a different
type of bait.
2 - Fish either deeper
or shallower in the
water column.

Escape The Pressure

Due to angling pressure, many fisheries are on the decline. Trophy bass, in particular, are more vulnerable during low waters and spawning times. Fishing pressure on some lakes is tremendous, and short of regulating the number of angler days to minimize constant use of their resource, little can be done from the management side.

Some of the most crowded waters are typically those that have just opened to the public. "Virgin" waters where bass have never seen a lure attract masses of anglers that find out a relatively new impoundment is no longer closed.

- Pressure in the initial days of newly-opened waters is often overwhelming, unless management measures are taken to prevent the devastation normally caused.

The initial stocking of bass in the typically new reservoir must provide the bass fishery for about the first five years. This is why "opening day" slaughters by crowds of eager anglers are so detrimental to a new bass fishery. The Texas Parks and Wildlife Department realized this after observing a couple of slaughters several years ago and have since taken corrective measures.

- A gradual increase in fishing pressure is desired; so often the news of a lake opening is by word of mouth rather than through the media.

Closed seasons, which a few states and some individual waters have, may reduce harvest if closed long enough and at the right time, but they don't reduce the crowds.

By closing a season you automatically create the "opening day." So again, slaughters can potentially occur.

Closures also have the undesirable effect of reducing fishing opportunity, which is contrary to many people's ideas on proper fish management. Thus, closed seasons have not gained widespread use around the country.

The type of restrictions proposed that could provide adequate protection for bass and maximum opportunity for anglers sometimes vary from biologist to biologist. The objectives of the length limit restrictions are obviously to increase the quality of fishing and the fisherman's catch rate. As some studies suggest, that may help reduce angler participation and heavy fishing pressure.

On a relatively small body of water, bass that aren't used to heavy boat traffic or fishing pressure, can be spooked even by a major tournament with several hundred contestants.

- The shallow water bass population is most affected. When things start to calm down, the bass will move out of their hiding places, but that might not be until the event is over.

- The fish may not come out of that fright until a day or two after the tournament.

Over a short period of time, pressured fish are on guard and more difficult to catch. Here are some tips:

- You need to be extremely quiet in your approach to any potential bass hangout.

- If possible, drift instead of using an electric motor.

- If you have to use the trolling motor, whether during the daylight or at night, don't do so any more than necessary.

If it's not possible to fish off-hours, then use some of the tactics described above to increase the catch when the crowds have spooked the bass. This significant intensity of anglers wishing to locate and catch largemouth bass is expected to continue for several more years.

Larry Larsen on Bass Tactics

CHAPTER 28

BEST LOCATIONS FOR DARK APPROACHES
Try these techniques to locate summer-night action

Explosions on the surface of the calm lake sounded more like alligator foraging than bass. Frogs and other night creatures were all there, doing their thing, and so was I. Sounds are amplified after dark, when an angler must rely on senses other than sight. I was quickly reminded of that.

My eyes hadn't fully adjusted to the darkness when a 6-pounder tried to steal my 8-inch worm. The thief made its way into submerged timber, but the line held as I pulled the fish out of the obstruction. The largemouth took to the sky and when it descended, sounded like a sure 10-pounder. A second jump closer to the net gave me a chance to eyeball the fish.

I brought the bass to the boat, carefully unhooking the lure from its mouth before releasing it. The fish was the first of 16 that my partner and I eventually caught and released during the night. From sundown to 3 a.m., we probed the edges of a 3-foot-deep spoil area using black plastic wigglers. The lake's main channel, approximately 20 feet deep, lay on one side of the spoil area; an 8-foot-deep flat lay on the other.

Our bass that night came from the top of the "hump", in proximity to the rapid drop. Texas-rigged worms were bounced down the drop and into the mouths of the bass. Largemouth were feeding on large insects and baitfish cruising just beneath the surface. Every now and then, the baitfish were swiping off a bug and the bass were not far behind.

Such baitfish are at a extreme disadvantage because of their poor night vision. Under bright sunlight conditions, they feed on plankton near the water's surface and are often able to avoid the predators. After dark, however, shiners and other minnows normally exhibit a severe case of night blindness. But this is not the case with deeper feeding bass whose eyes are accustomed to the dimmer light level.

Check Out The Area For Forage

Gourmet forage can be seen at night with the help of a good flashlight or spotlight. Shine the beam on the water's surface and you'll probably discover hundreds of frogs, freshwater eels and small bullhead catfish.

Another common night-active morsel, the crayfish, is definitely a nocturnal feeder. It hides under rocks during sunlight hours and explores the bottom after hours. Its incredibly poor eyesight makes it a prime target for the larger nocturnal-feeding predators.

You only have to run your boat across a lake after dark with a spotlight to see and experience insect life. Once you have scooted

Glistening moonlit lakes are often productive bass haunts. On unfamiliar waters, it's best to arrive prior to nightfall so that landmarks can be more easily determined.

through some bug "storms," you'll be picking insects out of your teeth for several minutes after you stop the boat. Both forage fish and bass love these conditions, and such a "find" is a great place to utilize your best nighttime approach.

Larry Larsen on Bass Tactics

How To Select The Best Lake For Moonlight Angling

After sunset, the most productive bass waters are generally the hardest to fish during daylight. In short, use the guise of darkness to an advantage. Bass feel more protected at night. How they react to noise differs:

- During the day, bass will approach a disturbing noise with caution.

- After dark, bass may approach with curiosity and interest.

A prime consideration in selecting the best lake for after-dark angling is how well you know the waters. Fish only the waters with which you are thoroughly familiar. Finding the precise location of bass hangouts in the darkness on a lake you know will be difficult enough.

A lake with heavy daytime pressure or boat traffic, especially in the form of water skiers, is usually a great night-fishing lake. Sunlight activity on such waters continually disturbs the best accessible fishing areas and creates night-feeding patterns. After the speed boaters have disappeared, bass become less wary and are overtaken by their hunger.

Don't Underestimate The Importance of Sighting and Sight

Whether you know the lake or not, as daylight fades, scan the landmarks in relation to distant lights as they are turned on. Under a full moon, you can see the shoreline and objects above water, but on a new moon, you and your partner are virtually blind without landmarks or artificial light of some sort.

Your partner is, of course, a welcome companion who provides a degree of additional safety. Darkness covers one another's presence and mistakes. Hopefully, none will be of the kind that requires help from the person at the other end of the boat.

- Clear-water lakes usually are more productive at night (see Chapters 6 and 7 for more information on these type bodies). A muddy lake may not be as gainful. Waters clear enough to drink from should be fished at night, since in the daytime, fish limit their movements. A successful angler, though, should use extreme stealth to be amply rewarded on a moonlit night.

- Many clear-water lakes, both large and small, fit into the superior night-waters category: Table Rock Lake in Missouri, Bull Shoals Lake in Arkansas, the Hill Country lakes in Texas, Lake Tenkiller and Grand Lake in Oklahoma, Wilson Reservoir in Kansas, Lake

To catch monster bass after dark you must treat lunar rays on bright moon-drenched nights as you would those of the sun. Many of the country's biggest bass are taken under a full moon. Check out the tips below to aid in your moonlight search.

- Guntersville in Alabama, West Point Lake in Georgia, Santee Cooper in South Carolina and East Lake Tohopekaliga and Lake Wier in Florida. Many others exist throughout the United States.

Lots of huge bass are taken at night from these types of waters. The Orange Lake, Florida, record bass of 17 pounds, 4 ounces caught by R.W. Campbell was taken on a black Jitterbug. Two state-record largemouth bass in Kentucky were taken after dark. The largest was caught at night from a very small lake using a plastic worm.

Where To Effectively Probe The Shallows

The shallows that produce small bass in the daytime often contain lunker bass in low light, so that locating them at night is generally easier. Under the cloak of darkness, bass move out of dense vegetation into and around the edges of their cover. They'll migrate along the deepest shadows into the shallows where they are susceptible.

On bright, moon-drenched nights, treat the lunar rays as you would those of the sun. To ambush their prey, bass hide in the shadows of structure and move along the shaded sides of cover.

- Points running from deep water and outside weed patches are good nocturnal habitat, as are boat lanes, weed lines, tree lines and shallow-dock pilings.

- Lighted piers and boat docks on popular residential-type lakes are great after dark spots (see Chapters 22 and 23 for more on docks). Many of the docks have submerged trees off the end which are often placed there for crappie. The lighted ones attract bugs and bass. The predator will stack up in such places, even in crystal-clear water only four feet deep.

- Boat docks with lights are great, but the double-wide boat houses painted white are equally bountiful. They are like big movie screens to bass, a night-fishing guide once told me. Largemouth will seek some source of light or pale-colored background to see the outline of their prey.

- Dark areas collect fish in daylight, light areas attract them on black nights. A white-sand beach is a good place to look, because swimmers' feet in the daytime kick up sediment off the bottom. Forage moves in to feed after the wet set has vacated the area. Bass can easily catch their prey over the white sand.

- Other areas with a light-colored bottom are good night-fishing spots. Shallow, sandy depressions or holes in heavy vegetation next to the bank attract huge largemouth under the low-light conditions.

Bass can totally utilize an extremely shallow area at night, whereas they may be "confined" to a deeper, sun-drenched point during the day. Bass will move around more at night than during daylight hours and are less dependent on good structure during moonless evenings.

Try The Rhythmic Retrieves For Maximum Action

When prospecting for night-prowling bass, your retrieve with the same monotonous cadence will outproduce all others. Rhythm

DARK APPROACHES BASED ON LUNAR ACTIVITY CONSIDERATIONS

On a full moon, when bass are able to see better during darkened hours, the retrieve speed may be faster.

On a dark moon, vision is limited for us and bass. Slow down lure speed.

is critical at night, regardless of the lure. The plain vanilla, steady pulsating retrieve will be your most effective method for largemouth. Too, you can cover more ground if you forget the fancy twitch and jerk retrieves.

Another way for you to increase productivity is to learn to set the hook at the right moment. By resisting the "big set" upon the resounding splash until you feel tension on the line, you will net more bass. It's best to wait an instant before you set the hook on a topwater lure. The bass that homes in on the sound, completely missing the plug, will come right back after it if still in the vicinity.

When it's quiet, you can hear the commotion easily. Fortunately, midnight-feeding bass prefer still water, so you can fish the protected banks out of the wind. The best ones lie in shallow water near a deep-water drop-off. Here's how to check out these spots:

- Around such topographical changes, fish mid-depth lures that are easily silhouetted against the moonlit sky.

- Make short, controllable casts, and then prepare for the exciting strikes that occur right at the boat when you least expect them.

Time Your Trip To The Lake For Night Time Thrills

Most successful night anglers have their own ideas about the best possible time to chase bass. They often chose their optimal time after sundown, depending on a couple of parameters: temperature and oxygen levels.

- Water temperature is a critical factor in any type of bass fishing. If the temperature is below 70 degrees, go early; and if it is above 90, try after midnight. Bass seem to be more active in hot water as their metabolism increases, but oxygen is also a key to the best time.

- Dissolved oxygen levels peak toward the end of the day and summer levels are big factors in bass feeding. Lower oxygen in weed beds after midnight may prohibit extensive activity until dawn. In winter, oxygen levels are less of a factor in bass activity.

Summer bass activity peaks earlier after sundown, also due to the night vision of the predator. The basic difference between our eyes and those of a bass is that ours normally adapt from brightness to darkness quicker. While it normally takes human eyes about 30 minutes to fully adapt to darkness, the night vision of bass, in cool water, could take a few hours.

Solunar influences also seem to have an impact on night angling. The three nights before a full moon and the three nights after are preferred by many nocturnal fishermen. The biggest bass, some anglers believe, are caught when the moon comes up in the late afternoon before the sun has gone down.

Nocturnal angling often can leave you with memorable experiences of tranquility and occasionally the largest bass of your life. Be alert to the grip of the rod and thumb pressure on the reel, and don't be lulled into a sleepy trance by the mesmerizing gurgle of a surface lure. You'll catch more lunker bass while fully awake.

Larry Larsen on Bass Tactics

CHAPTER 29

SIX NOCTURNAL WEED WAYS

Night fishing around vegetation is productive with these methods

After dark, anglers can sneak up on secluded bass haunts and coax fish to strike. The most difficult places to effectively fish during sun times are those with tremendous water clarity or dense vegetation. At night, however, these same places often yield largemouth.

Night fishing around vegetation is often productive, and concentrations of bass may be easy pickings for those employing the right methods. There are several effective ways to catch weed-bound bass after dark. Some of the most popular are the following:

Drifting Grass Spoons

On windy nights, drifting surface spoons over soft grasses is a deadly ploy. The optimal conditions include stained water, a new or dark moon, and heavy grass vegetation growing in three to seven feet of water. The most productive spoons have a design that allows them to ride the surface at a very slow pace. After dark, a boat can drift over dense grass patches such as pepper grass, sawgrass, or eel grass, and the lure can follow.

- To effectively fish the baits, the angler should hold the rod tip high, so that the lure is always on the surface. These baits are weedless and can be dragged through the most snag-infested weed beds around.

- The lure is most productive as it falls into pockets and/or rides across beds. You probably won't see a wake behind your lure, but you may hear the strike. Certainly, you'll feel it, if the fish connects.

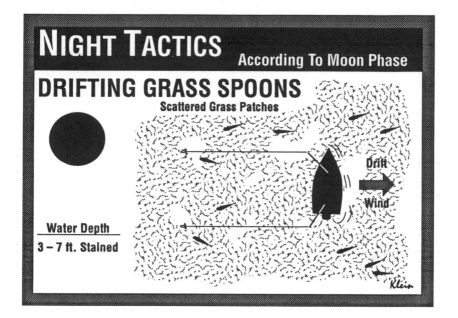

NIGHT TACTICS
According To Moon Phase

DRIFTING GRASS SPOONS
Scattered Grass Patches

Drift

Wind

Water Depth
3 – 7 ft. Stained

Klein

- In stained or roily waters, the spoon's sound is important, since visibility could be minimal. That sound is the main attractor under these conditions, and a paddle-wheel spoon is often a good choice for this method.

- A twitching of the rod during the drift will enticingly 'rock' the lure. Large bass, in particular, get excited by a dancing bait, and the surface may explode as a bass tries to get at the lure.

In general, the skitter-type spoon is the most effective tool for drifting dense grassy areas at night. A single hook and ability to ride the surface and hop over small obstructions is the key to this lure's productivity. Most of these lures are made of a hard plastic material making them light enough to work easily on the surface.

The design of the spoon makes the lure ride on its back with the hook riding up, away from the vegetation. That's vital to catching bass with spoons in almost total darkness.

Jig Flippin' The Perimeters

With an underhand cast, the after-hours angler can probe cover that's more difficult to fish with conventional methods during daylight. He can maneuver his boat in the heavy cover and

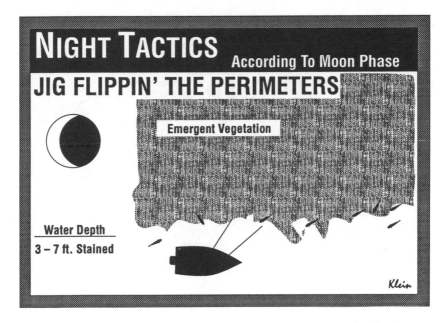

NIGHT TACTICS
According To Moon Phase
JIG FLIPPIN' THE PERIMETERS

Emergent Vegetation

Water Depth

3 – 7 ft. Stained

Klein

'sneak' to within a few feet of the bass that is secluded in the dense habitat. In pitchin' or flippin', the lure is seldom out of productive water.

- The night-time ploy of raising and lowering a jig is best utilized in stained waters with emergent vegetation such as cattails, reeds or rushes growing in four to seven feet of water. Some moonlight is needed so that the angler, standing near the trolling motor controls, can target the holes in the perimeter weedline.

- When manipulating the rod in heavy cover, excess line from the tip will easily become tangled. At night, this can be very frustrating. As you pull the line in, let it fall on the casting deck of the boat. It'll be out of the way of the heavy cover that surrounds the craft.

Flippin' is one effective technique that I've used on many waters around the country. I'll make sure that my line and rod are beefy for such night time exercise. That's usually a vital consideration.

Worming Weed Structures

The same structure that is productive during the day is usually more productive at night. Bigger bass are often found feeding on offshore structures, and a worm-tossing angler may find that he can successfully work shallower waters at night.

Six Nocturnal Weed Ways 189

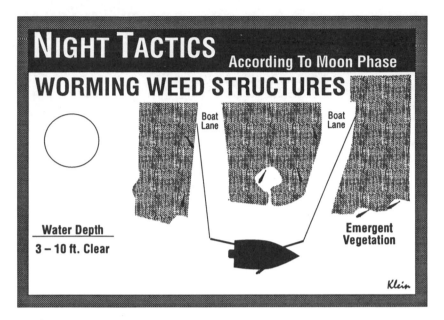

NIGHT TACTICS
According To Moon Phase
WORMING WEED STRUCTURES

Boat Lane

Boat Lane

Water Depth
3 – 10 ft. Clear

Emergent Vegetation

Klein

It isn't easy, though, to think of worming deeper structures at night, because most anglers prefer to work some slightly (at least) visible objects near shore.

- To the productive plastic worm fisherman, being able to find good deep-water structure is important. He may want to mark hot spots with floating marker buoys in the daylight or use lighted buoys at night.

- Bass generally move along the same routes at night that they do before dark. How far they'll travel depends on light, food and changes in weed terrain, but expect night movement to terminate closer to the shallows. Sharp breaks near shallows are prime night-time targets for an angler with a Texas-rigged worm.

- Many successful structure fishermen prefer full moon nights to dark nights. In July and August, anglers have noticed that exciting things can happen during the phase of the moon when it first begins to rise above the horizon and, again, when it falls below the far horizon.

- Structure-oriented bass will either turn on or turn off around these times. The lake's bass population may just disappear or decide that your worm, bumping along the submerged grass, could just be its last meal.

The best conditions for structure-worming are clear waters with intermittent vegetation patches along the bottom three to 10

Larry Larsen on Bass Tactics

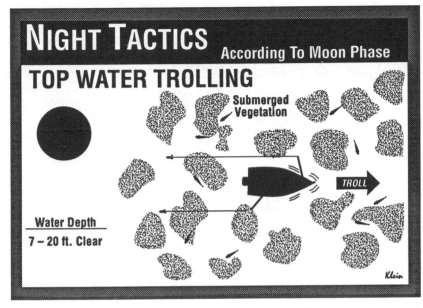

NIGHT TACTICS According To Moon Phase

TOP WATER TROLLING

Submerged Vegetation

TROLL

Water Depth
7 – 20 ft. Clear

Klein

feet deep. A worm tosser can most effectively fish boat lanes and troughs in vegetation after dark. The bait can also be dropped beside emergent weedbeds where bass often await forage.

Top Water Trolling

In very clear waters with submerged heavy weed-cover, a highly productive night-time technique consists of trolling a black Musky Jitterbug over the vegetation. The method works best in deeper water with little or no moon present. Several other types of surface lures can be also trolled via the electric motor, including those with spinners or cupped noses.

The advantage of the surface-trolled lure in heavy submerged weed cover is that it brings the bass to the top, making it easier for the angler to keep the bass head up and out of the entanglements below. Keeping big bass on the surface and out of trouble is the key to landing them at night.

Hydrilla, elodea, coontail and other submerged plant beds in seven to 20 feet of water offer prime locations to troll the top water fare. Although the aquatic weed growth may be abundant, hangups will seldom be a problem.

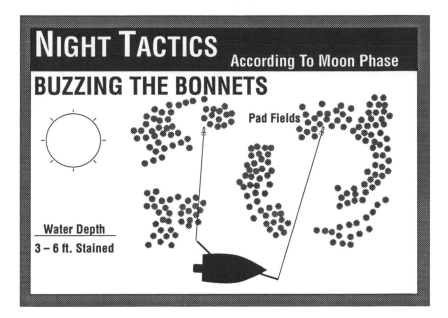

NIGHT TACTICS
According To Moon Phase
BUZZING THE BONNETS

Pad Fields

Water Depth
3 – 6 ft. Stained

Here are some guidelines for employing this method:

- Be on the water around the new moon to minimize the moving boat's impact on the darkened aquatic environment.

- Place the lines about 75 feet behind the boat and troll only two plugs at a time. Any more than that could cause problems after dark, such as entanglements with each other.

- Keep a strong grip on the trolling rod and be aware of any movement around the lure.

The productive angler will never set the hook at the sound of a splash near the bait; he will wait to feel tension in the line. When the lure stops moving along the surface, the angler either has a fish or a snag. Then, it's time to set the hook!

Buzzing The Bonnets

Retrieving your lure through a bed of lily pads at night takes practice. Under a full moon, watching the lure is important to determine snags from strikes. Casts should be made as short as practical and boat movement should be minimal to prevent hangups. The fringes of the bonnets ahead of the boat should be worked

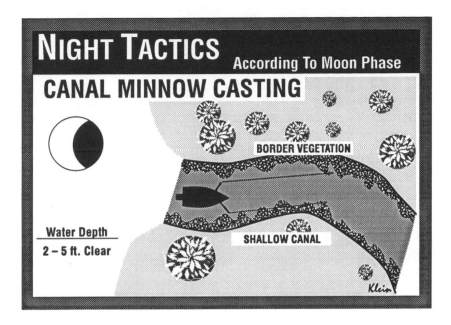

NIGHT TACTICS
According To Moon Phase
CANAL MINNOW CASTING

BORDER VEGETATION

Water Depth
2 – 5 ft. Clear

SHALLOW CANAL

Klein

first. This will allow a more taut line, which means better lure control and a better hook set when needed.

- Productive anglers toss in-line spinners and small buzz baits around expansive bonnet beds. For best action, lures should ride on or near the water's surface with the spinners churning it to a froth. Under a full moon, it may be easy to see pads moving as the bass bump the stems while moving about.

- This method works best when the pads are scattered over a large area and lie in three to six feet of water. I caught 10 bass, including one of six and one half pounds, from a bonnet bed one night, but it took time and patience. The lure is normally buzzed through pockets in the pads for greatest success.

- Bass may pop the bait without getting hooked, but that's the chance one takes in pad fishing at night. In denser pad beds, largemouth will have little time to look at the lure and may strike instinctively, missing their target. In less dense cover, bass often take the lure solidly.

While a big bass is particularly hard to land from a pad jungle at night, most anglers feel that provoking the strike should be the major consideration. Once that is accomplished, then landing the fish takes priority. Once the bass has struck, keep her on the surface and coming to you to prevent her from diving into the heavy stuff. A pork strip, pork frog, or rubber grub can often be added to this offering to increase its effectiveness.

Canal Minnow-Casting

In very clear water, shallow canals with border vegetation are difficult daytime fishing spots. After dark, such places can be very productive, under the right conditions. Some moonlight is needed - a half moon minimum - and water depth adjacent to the weedy border should be two to five feet.

- Casting minnow plugs along vegetation lines can be exciting. Whereas a slender subsurface lure may attract only a following wake during the day, the soft-landing lure will result in a smashing strike under the moon.

- The casts should be parallel to and ahead of the boat. The most productive lure will normally be twitched two or three times and then reeled steadily back.

- The boat should be positioned near the border vegetation, and electric motor use should be kept at a minimum. Use it to move 10 feet at a time and then shut off the electric. Coast another 10 feet, and cast the weed edges six or eight times before starting the trolling motor again.

You can find productive man-dug canals around boat basins, marinas, residential and commercial developments on many reservoirs and rivers. Anywhere on the water's perimeter where man requires access for whatever reason, there could be such a canal. Clear canals have man-made advantages over other deep clear waters. Due to a closer "association" with man, the tiny waterways (as described in chapters 8 and 9) have more nutrients and correspondingly greater vegetation. That often translates to more bass.

CHAPTER 30

PLAYING THE TEMPERATURE GAME
Water temperature wisdom can be applied year around

The importance of water temperature on my bass catches couldn't have been more enlightening. I had boated from a large, cold lake through a three-mile-long river channel to a smaller shallow body of water on the chain. My temperature gauge revealed a 5 degree difference and my plastic worms registered a similar result.

Seven bass from the warmer waters in the following hour made the winter-time trip worthwhile. I vowed from then on to note the temperature differences, particularly during the extreme temperature cycles that come and go with the seasons. Bass, of course, are in tune with their environment and its temperature.

It makes sense that thermal factors affect bass. Several water characteristics are linked to water temperature. Perhaps the primary one of interest to most fishermen is bass metabolism, the motivating factor in their lives.

Bass are cold-blooded, and as a result, their body temperature reflects that of the waters. Their activity level, in general, is linked to their metabolism and correspondingly, water temperature. Low temperatures generally result in a slow metabolic rate and high temperatures result in an increased rate.

Feeding and other energy expenditures occur at higher metabolic rates. Low temperatures usually result in slower digestive rates. For example, bass can digest a forage fish in about three days when the temperature is at 50 degrees, but it will only take one day when the temperature approaches 70 degrees.

Here are some other truths about water temperature influences:

- In extremely : cold waters (below 50 degrees), a bass may not feed more than once in a two-week period. Growth rates then are minimal, and bass may hold tighter to deep or dense cover.

- As a rule, bass in cold water will not chase after fast-moving baits.

- At water temperature levels above the mid- 80's (degrees F), much of that metabolic energy is consumed by life support rather than additional growth, however. They may feed twice a day, though, if other factors such as forage availability are suitable.

The "Optimal" Range And When To Look For It

Moderate temperatures seem to allow the bass maximum growth and generate foraging activity that is pleasing to anglers. Bass are active then and will chase lures being retrieved at most speeds. Although I've caught largemouth bass in waters with temperatures ranging from 45 to 95, an "optimum" water temperature range could probably be specified at 75 to 85. Not all bass will be found at locations within that range when it exists, just the majority.

- Various experiments and laboratory observations by fisheries biologists have concluded similar ranges, plus or minus five degrees, but bass may select the waters of a particular temperature out of that range for a brief period of time when feeding. For the most part however, they will move to the comfort provided in waters of the "optimum" range.

- With factors such as dissolved oxygen, structure, food and water quality being equal, game fish will seek a preferred or "optimal" temperature. The key words here are "being equal." All factors seldom are. Under different circumstances, the fish can be found in waters of widely varying temperatures.

Bass acclimation has a great influence on the precise temperature, as do the existing weather/lunar factors. In southern waters and heated power plant impoundments, bass may well be acclimated to a warmer "optimal" environment. They may respond to hormonal urges a little later and stay in waters with high temperatures (90 degrees) for long periods.

What Seasonal Variations In Temperatures Mean

Length of day (seasonal influences) and hormonal changes (spawning) apparently affect bass temperature preferences. Water temperature stability has a considerable effect on the bass. For

Larry Larsen on Bass Tactics

HOT WATER TROPHIES

"Big bass seek out cooler waters in the heat of the summer. It is not unusual for the author to catch 10-pound-plus trophies in Mid-August".

example, a daily fluctuation of more than 3 degrees is not usually accoptable to bass. A rapidly varying temperature can confuse a spawning fish. At that time and most others, largemouth will opt for a relatively stable temperature.

- In the spring, as days become longer and water temperatures move into the 60's, male bass begin to move toward spawning areas.

- Females follow as the temperature reaches 65 or so and the bedding soon takes place.

- Warmer waters above 75 to 80 degrees usually mean that bass will move farther after a lure and move after one being retrieved faster.

Anglers can cover water faster, and hopefully, develop a productive pattern quicker. The warmest water is usually on the surface, making a shallow approach better at times.

Temperature Parameters Which Influence Bass

The temperature of the lakes will vary with depth, as well as seasons of the year.

- In shallow waters, the change will be very little over nine or ten feet, usually only a degree or so.

- In larger, deeper bodies of water, the temperature may change greatly. Neither will the temperature be the same at any given depth in these larger bodies of water. Within these lakes, there are currents and other forms of stratification moving around.

Water temperature does make a difference to fish, because it also governs the dissolved oxygen content and regulates the food supply. This is understandable due to the fact that the dissolved oxygen content is, in general, inversely proportional to the water temperature. In order words, as the water temperature decreases, the amount of oxygen available for the fish increases and vice versa.

An excellent time to be on the lake is after a rainfall. The rainfall runoff reduces the water temperature but also carries in dissolved nutrients which reduce the dissolved oxygen content. Thus, there is an immediate drop in dissolved oxygen. While many factors influence catching fish after a rain shower, the prime one is the available food being washed in.

The nature of the runoff will determine the fluctuation of the temperature also. A higher reading will result from the watershed being from low, swampy land, while lower temperatures can be expected from a water-tumbling gully. Weather conditions before

198   *Larry Larsen on Bass Tactics*

Largemouth actively feed when their metabolism is high and the waters are warmer than others. Bass are closely attuned to the water temperature and dissolved oxygen content. Low light levels cause temperature to fluctuate by a few degrees.

and after a rain also are determining influences on the amount of bass you catch.

Check Out Warm Waters In Cold Weather

Finding warm waters on a bitter cold morning may be as easy as finding gentle river currents and deep water. River current and certain types of structure will hold some warmth on a sudden drop in temperature. Rocks, riprap and submerged trees or limbs will more commonly provide warmth to the water, and if they are found in a deep bend of the river with good current flow, they can hold good fish too.

I remember the 40-degree winter weather that had my friend tucking his ski mask into his snow suit before leaving the dock. The wind's chill at 40 miles per hour "cut" through our clothing and watered our eyes despite protective goggles. We soon were tossing lures toward a brushy river bank, however.

The current was brisk and submerged logs and trees were scattered all along and below the bank. My partner, braving the elements, took off one glove and began tossing his spinnerbait. A continual retrieve would provide some warmth. His fifth cast got him heated up quickly.

The lunker bass rolled behind the fallen tree limbs and dove into them, taking out drag at will. Soon, the fish became entangled and could take out no more line. Fortunately, the 14-pound monofilament held as we motored over to the snag. I grabbed the limb with gloved hand and gingerly lifted it, netting the bass when it came into view.

Usually, the first fish affected by low oxygen are the large game fish. Their oxygen requirements are heavier than those of small fish and rough fish. In general, though, warm water means bass. The fish feeding habits and activities are accelerated, and when you do find that water, it should help your catch.

A noticeable indicator of too high a water temperature may be fish activity in the area. Here's some of the signs:

Are fish frequently seen skimming the surface and are they gar or other rough fish?

• If you see no game fish activity, yet hear a lot of water "slapping" and notice rough fish suspended near the surface, then the area could have a high water temperature and be low in dissolved oxygen.

Check Out The Quality Of Water And These Tips

After a few years of weed control spraying, the sediment and sludge from the dying vegetation will build up and the depth of a lake will actually decrease. The resulting muck reduces the amount of water in the lake, allowing the temperature to increase to dangerous levels. This robs the water of oxygen and makes it uninhabitable for most species of fish.

In good quality water, a couple of tips might help you locate the better temperatures and the bass. They are:

• If you do locate a body of water with very high, fairly constant temperature readings, cast to deep water structure. The water there will most always be slightly cooler.

• If the water you are fishing is a very shallow lake or river, find shade and fish that. Such cover may provide a degree or two difference.

• The important measurable weather factor is the surface or near-surface water temperature. Monitor this key element with a temperature gauge. For the productive angler, a water temperature meter should have its place beside the pH meter and depth finder.

We later worked another shallower river bend with brush and each took a small keeper from it. Currents pushed 60-degree water against the bend allowing for a population of bass to exist there. Three bass apiece from the submerged logs in areas of current and deep water were our daily "warm" water reward. Very few other anglers caught anything in the 40-degree weather.

Not every winter day is like the one just mentioned, but many are a little cool for a relaxing, slow-casting day. There are several tactics you may want to employ under these circumstances:

1. A fairly active lure should be used, regardless of how fast it is fished.

2. If the water is too cold, a crankbait can be fished slow to catch the slower moving bass. Remember a couple of things here:

   - A plastic diving plug can be effectively slowed down.

   - Wood crankbaits, with more buoyancy, tend to be harder to control at slow, winter-time speeds.

The cold water will slow the bass metabolism down, and the lure must be presented slowly to take many bass. Fortunately, the winter weather slows down our metabolism also, so there isn't such a big adjustment to make. I've found bass will congregate in deeper, warm water areas in winter months when the water cools.

When Should You Look For Very Hot Water?

During the winter, most anglers observe the change in water temperature. But during the summer months, few consider that a factor in their success. They could be overlooking a key element, though, in bassing success.

Two of my better hot weather fishing days were in areas where the water temperature exceeded hot. On one of those days, I caught and released over 30 largemouth from runoff water which was cooler than the heated lake shallows. The following day, I was fishing a private lake with a water quality expert who measured the water temperature at several areas around the lake.

The latter experience was a special one-day fishing adventure on private waters at the invitation of the owner. My partner and I caught over 50 bass up to seven pounds in about five hours of casting. Water temperature approached 90 degrees in many areas that day.

- Don't assume, though, that the bass were not feeding in water 90 degrees. There are other parameters to consider before making that statement.. As the water temperature increases, fish become more active and this higher use of energy requires more food.

Several summers ago, I caught three very large bass from the St. John's River in Jacksonville, and the needle on my temperature gauge read 88-90+ degrees (the scale measured up to 90 degrees). All the fish were taken while they were lying in wait for passing baitfish beneath overhanging shade trees.

As I've explained, water temperatures increase to a certain point, which will speed up the fish metabolism and increase his activity. A feeding fish requires and uses more dissolved oxygen than a resting fish. Thus, it will not stay feeding in an area of high water temperature for long.

With a little water temperature wisdom, the extreme weather won't punish you so severely. You'll have company in the form of bass to warm you!

APPENDICES

Appendix A - About the Author

Appendix B - Resource Directory

Larry Larsen on Bass Tactics

APPENDIX A.

ABOUT THE AUTHOR

He's America's most widely read bass fishing writer and author. Larry Larsen is a frequent contributor on bass subjects to major outdoor magazines. More than 1,500 of Larsen's articles have appeared in magazines, including Outdoor Life, Sports Afield, Field & Stream, Bassin', North American Fisherman, Bass Fishing, Fishing Facts and Fishing Tackle Trade News. His photography has appeared on the covers of many national publications.

Larsen was recently called the "McDonalds of outdoor writers" by Sarasota Herald-Tribune writer Steve Gibson because "he keeps churning books out by what seems like thousands." It's true that Larsen has now authored 15 books on bass fishing and contributed chapters to another eight. They include the award-winning BASS SERIES LIBRARY, GUIDE TO FLORIDA BASS WATERS SERIES and others. He has also authored books on fishing opportunities in the Caribbean.

The Lakeland, FL based author is President of Larsen's Outdoor Publishing (LOP), the fastest growing publisher of outdoor titles in the country, and a member of the Outdoor Writers Association of America (OWAA), the Southeastern Outdoor Press Association (SEOPA), and the Florida Outdoor Writers Association (FOWA). Complete information on the author's other books and the LOP line of outdoor books can be found in the Resource Directory at the back of "Larry Larsen On Bass Tactics".

The author is not just a writer who has studied and written about all aspects of bass fishing for more than 20 years, he is an accomplished angler. As a result, his published works detail proven fish catching methods and special techniques. The avid fisherman carefully explains the latest and very best tactics to help readers find and catch bass anywhere. Larry works with several tackle companies on new lure and techniques development. His analysis of what works and why will help anyone catch more and bigger bass!

The avid bass angler for 35 years has caught and released hundreds of bass between five and 12 pounds. Larry Larsen has literally traveled the globe to fish for largemouth and the uncommon species of bass. He has fished lakes from Canada to Honduras and from Cuba to Hawaii. He is a former world record holder (Suwannee bass) and tournament professional. He lives on Highland Hills Lake in Central Florida about 30 feet from his bass boat and boat house.

BASS SERIES LIBRARY
by Larry Larsen

(BSL1) FOLLOW THE FORAGE VOL. 1 - BASS/PREY RELATIONSHIP - Learn how to determine dominant forage in a body of water and you will consistently catch more and larger bass.

(BSL2) VOL. 2 BETTER BASS ANGLING TECHNIQUES - Learn why one lure or bait is more successful than others and how to use each lure under varying conditions.

(BSL3) BASS PRO STRATEGIES - Professional fishermen know how changes in pH, water level, temperature and color affect bass fishing, and they know how to adapt to weather and topographical variations. Learn from their experience. Your productivity will improve after spending a few hours with this compilation of techniques!

(BSL4) BASS LURES - TRICKS & TECHNIQUES - When bass become accustomed to the same artificials and presentations seen over and over again, they become harder to catch. You will learn how to modify your lures and rigs and how to develop new presentation and retrieve methods to spark the interest of largemouth!

(BSL5) SHALLOW WATER BASS - Bass spend 90% of their time in the shallows, and you spend the majority of the time fishing for them in waters less than 15 feet deep. Learn productive new tactics that you can apply in marshes, estuaries, reservoirs, lakes, creeks and small ponds, and you'll likely triple your results!

(BSL6) BASS FISHING FACTS - Learn why and how bass behave during pre- and post-spawn, how they utilize their senses when active and how they respond to their environment, and you'll increase your bass angling success! By applying this knowledge, your productivity will increase for largemouth as well as redeye, Suwannee, spotted and other bass species!

(BSL7) TROPHY BASS - If you're more interested in wrestling with one or two monster largemouth than with a "panful" of yearlings, then learn what techniques and locations will improve your chances. This book takes a look at geographical areas and waters that offer better opportunities to catch giant bass. You'll also learn proven lunker-bass-catching techniques for both man-made and natural bodies of water!

(BSL8) ANGLER'S GUIDE TO BASS PATTERNS - Catch bass every time out by learning how to develop a productive pattern quickly and effectively. "Bass Patterns" is a reference source for all anglers, regardless of where they live or their skill level. Learn how to choose the right lure, presentation and habitat under various weather and environmental conditions!

(BSL9) BASS GUIDE TIPS - Learn secret techniques known only in a certain region or state that often work in waters all around the country. It's this new approach that usually results in excellent bass angling success. Learn how to apply what the country's top guides know!

Nine Great Volumes To Help You Catch More and Larger Bass!

LARSEN ON BASS SERIES

(LB1) LARRY LARSEN ON BASS TACTICS is the ultimate "how-to" book that focuses on proven productive methods. It is dedicated to serious bass anglers - those who are truly interested in learning more about the sport and in catching more and larger bass each trip. Hundreds of highlighted tips and drawings explain how you can catch more and larger bass in waters all around the country. This reference source by America's best known bass fishing writer will be invaluable to both the avid novice and expert angler!

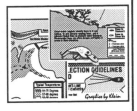

BASS WATERS SERIES
by Larry Larsen

Take the guessing game out of your next bass fishing trip. The most productive bass waters in each Florida region are described in this multi-volume series, including boat ramps, seasonal tactics, water characteristics and much more. Both popular and overlooked locations are detailed with numerous maps and photos. The author has lived and fished extensively in each region of the state over the past 25 years.

(BW1) GUIDE TO NORTH FLORIDA BASS WATERS - Covers from Orange Lake north and west. Includes Lakes Orange, Lochloosa, Talquin and Seminole, the St. Johns, Nassau, Suwannee and Apalachicola Rivers and many more of the region's best! You'll learn where bass bite in Keystone Lakes, Newnans Lake, St. Mary's River, Doctors Lake, Black Creek, Juniper Lake, Ortega River, Lake Jackson, Lake Miccosukee, Chipola River, Deer Point Lake, Blackwater River, Panhandle Mill Ponds and many more!

(BW2) GUIDE TO CENTRAL FLORIDA BASS WATERS - Covers from Tampa/Orlando to Palatka. Includes Lakes George, Rodman, Monroe, Tarpon and the Harris Chain, the St. Johns, Oklawaha and Withlacoochee Rivers and many others! You'll find the best spots to fish in the Ocala Forest, Crystal River, Hillsborough River, Conway Chain, Homosassa River, Lake Minneola, Lake Weir, Lake Hart, Spring Runs and many more!

(BW3) GUIDE TO SOUTH FLORIDA BASS WATERS - Covers from I-4 to the Everglades. Includes Lakes Tohopekaliga, Kissimmee, Okeechobee, Poinsett, Tenoroc and Blue Cypress, the Winter Haven Chain and many more! You'll learn where bass can be caught in Fellsmere Farm 13. Caloosahatchee River, Lake June-in-Winter, Lake Hatchineha, the Everglades, Lake Istokpoga, Peace River, Crooked Lake, Lake Osborne, St. Lucie Canal, lake Trafford, Shell Creek, Lake Marian, Myakka River, Lake Pierce, Webb Lake and many more!

> For more than 20 years, award-winning author Larry Larsen has studied and written about bass fishing. His angling adventures are extensive, from Canada to Honduras and from Cuba to Hawaii. He is Florida Editor for *Outdoor Life* and contributor to all major outdoor magazines.

OUTDOOR TRAVEL SERIES
by Larry Larsen and M. Timothy O'Keefe

Candid guides with inside information on the best charters, time of the year, and other important recommendations that can make your next fishing and/or diving trip much more enjoyable.

(OT1) FISH & DIVE THE CARIBBEAN - Vol. 1 Northern Caribbean, including Cozumel, Cayman Islands, The Bahamas, Jamaica, Virgin Islands and other popular destinations. Required reading for fishing and diving enthusiasts who want to know the most cost-effective means to enjoy these Caribbean islands. You'll learn how to select the best destination and plan appropriately for your specific interests.

(OT3) FISH & DIVE FLORIDA & The Keys - Includes in-depth information on where and how to plan a vacation to America's most popular fishing and diving destination. Special features include artificial reef loran numbers; freshwater springs/caves; coral reefs/barrier islands; gulf stream/passes; inshore flats/channels; and back country estuaries.

(OT2) FISH & DIVE THE CARIBBEAN - Vol. 2 - *COMING SOON!* Southern Caribbean, including Guadeloupe, Costa Rica, Venezuela, other destinations.

"Fish & Dive the Caribbean, Vol. 1" was one of four finalists in the Best Book Content Category of the National Association of Independent Publishers 1991 competition. Over 500 books were submitted by various U.S. publishers, including Simon & Schuster and Turner Publishing, Inc. Said the NAIP judges "An excellent source book with invaluable instructions for fishing or diving. Written by two nationally-known experts who, indeed, know what vacationing can be!"

DIVING SERIES
by M. Timothy O'Keefe

(DL1) DIVING TO ADVENTURE will inform and entertain novice and experienced divers alike with its in-depth discussion of how to get the most enjoyment from diving and snorkeling. Aimed at divers around the country, the book shows how to get started in underwater photography, how to use current to your advantage, how to avoid seasickness, how to dive safely after dark, and more. Special sections detail how to plan a dive vacation, including live-aboard diving.

M. Timothy O'Keefe was editor of the first major dive travel guidebook published in the U.S. The award-winning author writes for numerous diving, travel and sportfishing publications.

COASTAL FISHING GUIDES

(FG1) FRANK SARGEANT'S SECRET SPOTS - Tampa Bay to Cedar Key - A unique "where-to" book of detailed secret spots for Florida's finest saltwater fishing. This guide book describes little-known honeyholes and tells exactly how to fish them. Prime seasons, baits and lures, marinas and dozens of detailed maps of the prime spots are included. A comprehensive index helps the reader to further pinpoint productive areas and tactics.

(FG2) FRANK SARGEANT'S SECRET SPOTS -Southwest Florida
COMING SOON!!

INSHORE SERIES
by Frank Sargeant

(IL1) THE SNOOK BOOK-"Must" reading for anyone who loves the pursuit of this unique sub-tropic species. Every aspect of how you can find and catch big snook is covered, in all seasons and all waters where snook are found.

(IL2) THE REDFISH BOOK-Packed with expertise from the nation's leading redfish anglers and guides, this book covers every aspect of finding and fooling giant reds. You'll learn secret techniques revealed for the first time. After reading this informative book, you'll catch more redfish on your next trip!

(IL3) THE TARPON BOOK-Find and catch the wily "silver king" along the Gulf Coast, north through the mid-Atlantic, and south along Central and South American coastlines. Numerous experts share their most productive techniques.

(IL4) THE TROUT BOOK -Jammed with tips from the nation's leading trout guides and light tackle anglers. For both the old salt and the rank amateur who pursue the spotted weakfish, or seatrout, throughout the coastal waters of the Gulf and Atlantic.

Frank Sargeant is a renown outdoor writer and expert on saltwater angler. He has traveled throughout the state and Central America in pursuit of all major inshore species. Sargeant is Outdoor Editor of the Tampa Tribune and a Senior Writer for *Southern Saltwater* and *Southern Outdoors* magazines.

HUNTING LIBRARY
by John E. Phillips

(DH1) MASTERS' SECRETS OF DEER HUNTING - Increase your deer hunting success significantly by learning from the masters of the sport. New information on tactics and strategies for bagging deer is included in this book, the most comprehensive of its kind.

(DH2) THE SCIENCE OF DEER HUNTING - Covers why, where and when a deer moves and deer behavior. Find the answers to many of the toughest deer hunting problems a sportsman ever encounters!

(TH1) MASTERS' SECRETS OF TURKEY HUNTING - Masters of the sport have solved some of the most difficult problems you will encounter while hunting wily longbeards with bows, blackpowder guns and shotguns. Learn the 10 deadly sins of turkey hunting and what to do if you commit them.

FISHING LIBRARY

(CF1) MASTERS' SECRETS OF CRAPPIE FISHING by John E. Phillips - Learn how to make crappie start biting again once they have stopped, how to select the color of jig to catch the most and biggest crappie, how to find crappie when a cold front hits and how to catch them in 100-degree heat as well as through the ice. Unusual but productive crappie fishing techniques are included. Whether you are a beginner or a seasoned crappie fisherman, this book will improve your catch!

OUTDOOR ADVENTURE LIBRARY
by Vin T. Sparano, Editor-in-Chief, <u>Outdoor Life</u>

(OA1) HUNTING DANGEROUS GAME -It's a special challenge to hunt dangerous game - those dangerous animals that hunt back! Live the adventure of tracking a rogue elephant, surviving a grizzly attack, facing a charging Cape buffalo and driving an arrow into a giant brown bear at 20 feet. These classic tales will make you very nervous next time you're in the woods!

(OA2) GAME BIRDS & GUN DOGS - A unique collection of stories about hunters, their dogs and the upland game and waterfowl they hunt. These tales are about those remarkable shots and unexplainable misses. You will read about good gun dogs and heart-breaking dogs, but never about bad dogs, because there's no such animal.

LARSEN'S OUTDOOR PUBLISHING

CONVENIENT ORDER FORM

ALL PRICES INCLUDE POSTAGE/HANDLING

FRESH WATER

___ BSL3. Bass Pro Strategies ($14.95)
___ BSL4. Bass Lures/Tech. ($14.95)
___ BSL5. Shallow Water Bass ($14.95)
___ BSL6. Bass Fishing Facts ($13.95)
___ BSL8. Bass Patterns ($14.95)
___ BSL9. Bass Guide Tips ($14.95)
___ CF1. Mstrs' Scrts/Crappie Fshg ($12.95)
___ CF2. Crappie Tactics ($12.95)
___ CF3. Mstr's Secrets of Catfishing ($12.95)
___ LB1. Larsen on Bass Tactics ($15.95)
___ PF1. Peacock Bass Explosions! ($16.95)
___ PF2. Peacock Bass & Other Fierce
          Exotics ($17.95)
___ PF3. Peacock Bass Addiction ($18.95)

SALT WATER

___ IL1. The Snook Book ($14.95)
___ IL2. The Redfish Book ($14.95)
___ IL3. The Tarpon Book ($14.95)
___ IL4. The Trout Book ($14.95)
___ SW1. The Reef Fishing Book ($16.45)
___ SW2. Masters Bk/Snook ($16.45)

REGIONAL

___ FG1. Secret Spots-Tampa Bay/
          Cedar Key ($15.95)
___ FG2. Secret Spots - SW Florida ($15.95)
___ BW1. Guide/North Fl. Waters ($16.95)
___ BW2. Guide/Cntral Fl.Waters ($15.95)
___ BW3. Guide/South Fl.Waters ($15.95)
___ OT3. Fish/Dive Florida/ Keys ($13.95)

HUNTING

___ DH1. Mstrs' Secrets/ Deer Hunting ($14.95)
___ DH2. Science of Deer Hunting ($14.95)
___ DH3. Mstrs' Secrets/Bowhunting ($12.45)
___ DH4. How to Take Monster Bucks ($13.95)
___ TH1. Mstrs' Secrets/ Turkey Hunting ($14.95)

OTHER OUTDOORS BOOKS

___ DL2. Manatees/Vanishing ($11.45)
___ DL3. Sea Turtles/Watchers' ($11.45)

FREE BROCHURES

___ Peacock Bass Brochure
___ LOP Book Catalog

BIG MULTI-BOOK DISCOUNT!

2-3 books, SAVE 10%

4 or more books, SAVE 20%

INTERNATIONAL AIRMAIL ORDERS

Send check in U.S. funds; add $6 more for 1 book, $4 for each additional book

---

ALL PRICES INCLUDE U.S. POSTAGE/HANDLING

No. of books _____   x $_____ ea   = $_____
No. of books _____   x $_____ ea   = $_____
   Multi-book Discount   (%) $_____
SUBTOTAL $_____

☐ **Priority Mail (add $2.50 more for every 2 books)** $_____
TOTAL ENCLOSED (check or money order) $_____

*NAME*_____ *ADDRESS*_____

*CITY*_____ *STATE*_____ *ZIP* _____

***Send check/Money Order to: Larsen's Outdoor Publishing,
Dept. BR99, 2640 Elizabeth Place, Lakeland, FL 33813***
(Sorry, no credit card orders)

WRITE US!

If our books have helped you be more productive in your outdoor endeavors, we'd like to hear from you! Let us know which book or series has strongly benefited you and how it has aided your success or enjoyment. We'll listen.

We also might be able to use the information in a future book. Such information is also valuable to our planning future titles and expanding on those already available.

Simply write to Larry Larsen, Publisher, Larsen's Outdoor Publishing, 2640 Elizabeth Place, Lakeland, FL 33813.

We appreciate your comments!

Larry Larsen

OUTDOOR SPORTS SHOWS, CLUB SEMINARS and IN-STORE PROMOTIONS

Over the course of a year, most of our authors give talks, seminars and workshops at trade and consumer shows, expos, book stores, fishing clubs, department stores and other places. Please try to stop by and say hi to them. Bring your book by for an autograph and some information on secret new hot spots and methods to try. At these events, we always have our newest books, so come and check out the latest information. If you know of an organization that needs a speaker, contact us for information about fees. We can be reached at 813-644-3381. At our autograph parties, we talk "outdoors" and how to enjoy it to the fullest!

CONGRATULATIONS!...

on completing this "course" in bass tactics. You should have learned many things to apply on the next bass fishing trip. Keep in touch, as we have a tremendous library of fishing information to further enhance your success. We are bringing out numerous new outdoor titles every few months, so there are ongoing opportunities for you to prosper by our new "relationship".

CALL YOUR LIBRARY, BOOKSTORES & OUTDOOR SHOPS

Call or write your local library and recommend they stock "Larry Larsen On Bass Tactics" and our entire line of outdoor books. Ask your local bookstores and outdoor shops to do the same, and you'll have the best selection of informative books anywhere! For those readers who help us spread our distribution, we have a nice surprise. If your source orders their initial stock (five book minimum order) direct from us at LOP (and you let us know who you referred our books to), we will send you a FREE book. If your library orders only one title direct from us, we will still send you one of our special reports free. We appreciate your efforts on our behalf. - Larry Larsen

---

PERSONAL MAP CONSULTATION SERVICE

Larry Larsen will help you figure out where the bass are in your favorite lake or large river. For only $10, he will personally mark up any topo map you wish to send him. His suggestions will be based on the time of year you wish to fish that body of water. Include the date of the trip, expected water clarity and a detailed map with topographical lines (depth contours). The marked map will be returned within three weeks with a brief description of what you should try on the spots marked.

Save Money On Your Next Outdoor Book!

Because you've purchased a Larsen's Outdoor Publishing Book, you can be placed on our growing list of **preferred customers.**

You can receive special discounts on our wide selection of Outdoor Libraries and Series, written by our expert authors.

PLUS...

Receive Substantial Discounts for Multiple Book Purchases

AND...

Advance notices on upcoming books!

Yes, put my name on your mailing list to receive

1. Advance notice on upcoming outdoor books
2. Special discount offers

Name_____

Address_____

City, State, Zip_____

Index

C

cadence 183
camouflage 48
canal 60, 63, 64, 72, 73,
    75, 77, 79, 194
  circulating 39
  intake 38
Canal Minnow-Casting 194
canepoles 148
canoe 26, 64
canopy 5, 17, 18, 22, 23
carpet pieces 148
cattails 25, 30, 189
catwalks 77
channel bends 152
chart recorder 43, 96,
    98, 100, 153, 162
chest-high waders 118
clear water 5, 7, 14, 35,
    45-55, 154, 181, 194
closed seasons 176
Coast Guard-approved
    regulations 124
cold day 42
cold front 5, 37-43, 151, 152
cold night 44
cold water 37, 38, 44, 53,
    196, 201
cold weather 37-43, 69, 111,
    152, 199
Color-C-Lector 57
Combo-C-Lector 160, 162
coontail *(see moss)*
coot 23
country clubs 75, 81
cove 68
crankbait 36, 51-54, 65, 72, 83,
    93, 98-102, 110, 134, 138,
    143, 158, 165, 174, 201
crayfish 18, 20, 45, 53, 54,
    90, 138, 180
creature considerations 15
Creature Hazards 122
creeks 14, 24, 32, 37, 40, 42,
    60, 64, 66, 68, 78, 90,
    94, 100, 109, 110, 111
    116, 117, 120, 157, 165

crowds, tournament 168
crowded waters 7, 15, 167-171,
    174, 176
crustaceans, 45
current 20, 77, 83, 87, 90, 94,
    131, 133, 134, 136, 198, 199
cuts 20, 87, 90, 105, 126, 160
cypress trees 61

D

dam 15, 39, 126, 128, 133
dam tailrace 136
dark approach 7, 15, 16, 48,
    179-185
daytime pressure *(see pressure)*
deep sinks 77
deep water 14, 24, 37-44, 77,
    154, 199, 200
depth finder 98, 100, 163, 200
development waters 7, 14, 65,
    75, 78, 79, 81, 194
discharges 15, 38, 137
dissolved oxygen 162, 196,
    198, 199, 202
ditches 66
dock walking 143
docks 141, 145, 147, 149, 150
dog-days 151
downsizing 54
drag 41
drift, backwards 84
drop baits 91, 93
dropoff 42, 70, 77, 79, 111,
    142, 152, 185
duckweed 14, 17, 18

E

eddies 133, 136
eel grass 107, 187
eels, rubber 54
egrets 23
elodea 191
emergent vegetation 5, 14,
    24-29
environment 7, 36, 48, 49,
    51, 110, 159, 162

Larry Larsen on Bass Tactics

P

R

S